FELICIA CARTRIGHT

AND THE
SAD-EYED GIRL

Felicia   Joan

FELICIA CARTRIGHT

AND THE
SAD-EYED GIRL

BERNARD PALMER

ANEKO
PRESS

Aneko Press *Youth*

www.anekopress.com

Aneko Press, Life Sentence Publishing, and our logos are trademarks of
Life Sentence Publishing, Inc.
203 E. Birch Street
P.O. Box 652
Abbotsford, WI 54405

JUVENILE FICTION / Religious / Christian / Action & Adventure

Paperback ISBN: 979-8-88936-316-3

eBook ISBN: 979-8-88936-317-0

10   9   8   7   6   5   4   3   2   1

Available where books are sold

CONTENTS

CHAPTER 1

THE SAD-EYED GIRL

Slowly, Felicia Cartright raised her eyes and stared across sparkling Silver Lake snuggled gemlike in a mountain of green. Beyond the trees and an occasional boulder that lined the shore, a mountain fell away sharply to the valley below. For the moment, her best friend, Joan Bailey, and their young charges from the Rutledge Mountain Resort didn't exist. She was alone in the vast expanse of wilderness. She had seen more majestic mountains, that was true, and cliffs that were more sheer, more forbidding. But there was a restfulness in the scene around her, a tranquility that seemed to envelop her very being. She felt as though she wanted to stand there always, enjoying the beauty of what she saw.

But that was not to be. There was an impatient tug at her fingers.

"Miss Cartright."

At first, Felicia did not respond. It was as though she scarcely heard the young voice.

"Miss Cartright?" The nine-year-old at her side was more insistent.

Dimly, she became aware of him.

"Yes?"

"Would this be all right?"

She looked down at the stubby fingers that were firmly clamped on the tail of a tiny writhing garter snake.

"Oh!" Involuntarily, she screamed and jumped backward.

Disappointment gleamed in the boy's brown eyes as he saw that she was like most other girls when it came to fascinating objects like the one he held.

"It's just a little garter snake," he protested. "He's not going to hurt anybody."

Felicia was staring warily at the twisting, turning little reptile that seemed to raise its head every now and then to look at her. It was all she could do to keep from retreating.

"You never did hear of anybody who's been hurt by a little old baby garter snake, did you?"

"Probably not." With effort, she was able to keep precarious control of her voice. "But when Joan and I said we would like to prepare a nature display for parents' night we–" In spite of herself, she shuddered. "We had something else in mind."

But he was not willing to give up so easily.

"A little old garter snake is 'nature,'" he said. "And all those girls wouldn't even *touch* one." With a disdainful jerk of his head, he indicated Joan's team, which was made up chiefly of girls. "With this garter snake, we'll win, easy."

He moved forward, and she retreated, half a step at a time.

"But wouldn't–wouldn't that be taking an unfair advantage of them?"

"Because they wouldn't touch a little garter snake? Naw!"

"I–I just don't think we ought to have a garter snake in our display, Donald. I don't think he would be quite suitable." She was still inching backward, trying to put as much space between herself and the snake as possible without hurting Donald's feelings. "Now, why don't you take him over there and let him loose."

The tone in her voice showed him that he had lost the argument decisively. Reluctantly and still protesting, he did as he was told.

Felicia sighed in relief.

"Now, Donald, why don't you see if you can find some nice specimens of ferns or pine cones?"

"Aw–" He turned away. "I was figuring on finding some tadpoles."

"There aren't any tadpoles up here," she said, "are there?"

He brightened. "Can I look for some?"

Before waiting for an answer, he went scampering away. She watched him warily, trying to remember from her own somewhat tortured study of biology if there would be tadpoles in the area where they were.

She was still wondering about it when Joan came over to her.

"Well," she said brightly, "how's it going with your kids?"

"It was all right until a minute ago." Felicia shuddered.

"You don't mean that little garter snake, do you?"

Felicia's eyes narrowed accusingly.

"A little garter snake never hurt anybody," her friend continued.

"Joan Bailey!" she exploded. It was only with effort that she was able to keep her voice low enough so the little group of six-to-twelve-year-olds they were taking care of for the Rutledge Mountain Resort would not hear them. "I should have known that you were the one behind Donald's bringing that garter snake over to me!"

Her friend's laughter trilled. "I didn't *tell* him to bring that little garter snake to you. I just happened to see it."

"And pointed it out to him," Felicia concluded.

"Now that you mention it, I did get to talking to Donald and let it slip that I had seen this garter snake, but it wouldn't do my side any good because my girls would all be afraid to pick it up."

"Joan Bailey! You just wait! I'll get even with you!" she promised darkly.

"You'll have to admit that Donald did liven up the afternoon for you." Joan glanced at her watch. "We'd better be getting back, hadn't we? It's only an hour and a half until dinner time."

Felicia's attention was drawn to a slight, red-haired girl eleven or twelve years old. She looked as though she should have been smiling, that laughter was more at home in her soft blue-green eyes and on her pert little mouth than the frown that had been there ever since she joined the little group that morning.

This was the first nature hike Felicia and Joan had held, and the kids responded enthusiastically, dashing about to gather specimens of plant life on the mountain slope. All, that was, except the newcomer. She had been standing motionless since Felicia became aware of her, staring moodily at the ground.

"What's her name, Joan?" she asked in an undertone. "Do you remember?"

Joan shook her head.

Felicia approached the girl easily, as though she had known her all her life.

"Hi."

The girl raised her head slowly, eyeing Felicia with an arrogance that suggested she ought to go away and leave her alone.

"You're new here, aren't you?" Felicia ignored the unfriendliness in the child's glance.

"I came in with my dad last night."

"Oh, yes. I thought I should have recognized you. Mrs. Rutledge brought you over and introduced you to Joan and me last night."

The girl's head bobbed slightly in agreement.

"I'm Felicia Cartright. I probably have your name on my list, but I don't recall it without looking."

"I'm Mitzi Simmons." The girl spoke reluctantly as though it hurt to do so.

She would have turned away from Felicia, but the older girl moved with her easily. She asked Mitzi if she had met the other kids and if she was having fun. She answered in the affirmative but without enthusiasm.

"You came at an exciting time," Felicia continued. "We're gathering specimens for our nature display."

"I know."

"Why don't you and I look for something? What would you like to find?"

"I don't care about finding anything."

"You don't?"

"I think it's stupid!"

With that, she whirled on her heel and stormed away, but not before Felicia saw the tears quivering behind her eyelashes.

Joan saw what had happened.

"What was that all about?" she asked.

Felicia was near tears herself. "I wish I knew."

She wanted to follow Mitzi, to put her arm around

her and talk to her, to find out what was troubling her if she could, but something stopped her. To approach Mitzi now, she knew instinctively, would not be wise.

She tried not to be looking directly at the new girl in case she turned quickly and caught her, but she could not altogether keep from watching. Mitzi shuffled a few steps away, her head down. Then, as though undecided as to whether or not she should take part in helping collect the nature display, she picked up a leaf, examined it momentarily, and threw it away.

Felicia was still thinking about her when she and Joan went to their room to get ready for bed that night.

"I'm disturbed about Mitzi Simmons, Joan," she said suddenly.

Joan kicked off her shoes and looked up. "I'm not surprised."

"She's such an unhappy child."

"I don't get that picture of her at all," Joan countered. "If you ask me, I think she's spoiled rotten. She probably wanted to go somewhere else for her vacation, so she's determined not to enjoy a minute of her stay with us."

Felicia sat on the stool in front of the dresser, pensive. "I don't think so. There's something troubling her, Joan. She has the saddest eyes I've ever seen!"

CHAPTER 2

A SUMMER JOB

Felicia and Joan hadn't planned on going to the Rutledge Mountain Resort in South Dakota's Black Hills to work that summer. In fact, they had never even heard of the place. That, in itself, wasn't surprising. When the vacation jobs were posted on the bulletin board at Wellington School for Girls, they looked only as far down the list as those available in Yellowstone Park. There were a few jobs open in other places, but the list at Yellowstone was long and varied.

"Working in the park sounds so exciting," Joan exclaimed, excitement kindling in her voice. "And everyone says that the tips are fantastic."

Felicia read the list aloud once more. They needed waitresses, receptionists, cleaning girls, and clerks at the refreshment and souvenir stands, in addition to other workers.

In their room a few minutes later, they continued the discussion. "It sounds better than anything else that's offered this summer," Felicia observed.

"And we don't want to forget that there are as many boys who go to Yellowstone to work as there are girls."

The corners of Felicia's mouth tugged upward into a sly grin.

"Now the truth comes out. And you, a proper Wellington girl too. Miss Duncan is going to think that you are completely shameless."

"Miss Duncan!" Joan grimaced. "I don't think she was ever a girl herself."

"She didn't go running off to Yellowstone Park looking for boys, that's for sure. She was a proper, well-educated young lady. You should be ashamed of yourself."

Joan dropped to the chair at her desk.

"Of course, you realize that it isn't for myself that I'm concerned about getting where the boys are. I'm only thinking of you, Felicia. I know how heartbroken you would be if you had to be in a place where there weren't any boys."

"Don't try to put the blame on me. I know all about you. I know how allergic you are to guys."

Joan groaned in mock agony. "You've cut me. You've cut me to the quick, Felicia. And after all I have sacrificed for you, my best friend."

They looked at each other.

"Now I'm the one who's hurt," Felicia said. "I suppose the only thing I can do to get things straightened out is to agree to go to Yellowstone Park with you."

They went over the list of openings once more, decided on Yellowstone Park, and the next morning, as soon as the office that handled summer employment was open, they hurried down. Half a dozen girls were already there standing in line. Felicia and Joan joined them.

"I don't see why we have to apply through the school," Joan complained. "I'll bet the kids at other places apply directly."

"But that's not the way Miss Duncan does it," the girl in front of them said, sounding exactly like the precise dean of women. "That's not proper Wellington procedure. We have agreed to provide a given number of applicants. We must be certain that the correct number of girls write about working at those places that come to us for workers."

"I just know that we're too late," Joan said, chafed. "Everybody is going to want to go to Yellowstone Park if they can. We're not going to have a chance."

It only took a moment or two for each girl to record her name at the office and to be handed an application blank. They were next in line at the office when Miss Duncan came clicking down the corridor, her proper Wellington shoes clicking an efficient, businesslike beat as she moved briskly in the direction of her office. She started by, saw Joan standing there, and spun on her heel.

"Miss Bailey," she said crisply. "I just sent someone up to your room looking for you."

"For me?" Joan's eyes widened, silently asking Miss Duncan what she had done this time.

"I sent her to tell you that I want to see you. Please come to my office immediately."

Joan hesitated. "You mean right now?"

"Immediately." Miss Duncan's eyes flashed. "You know that a Wellington girl is to obey an order from her superiors without delay."

"But–but–Miss Duncan," Joan spluttered, "I've been standing in line for my turn to go in and see about a summer job."

"That can wait," she announced crisply. The dean of women ended the conversation abruptly by turning and stalking into her office where she stood at the door glaring in Joan's direction.

Joan glanced helplessly at Felicia and followed Miss Duncan. There was nothing else she could do.

Felicia stared after her uncertainly. The girl ahead of her came out of the office.

"You're lucky, Felicia," she said. "The quota for Yellowstone is almost filled."

That was what she was afraid of. If she went in and signed up for Yellowstone, she might have to go there alone. There was a good chance now that Joan wouldn't make it. Reluctantly, she turned away.

She waited uneasily in their room for Joan to come back. She tried to study, but kept looking at her watch with growing apprehension. If Joan hurried, there might be a chance. But it was almost time for their first morning class before Joan came back.

"What was it this time?" Felicia asked her.

She shrugged. "Oh, the usual. Miss Potter has my name on the down list because my history term paper isn't in yet."

Felicia sighed wearily. She had been reminding Joan about that term paper for the last month and a half.

"You know you could have had it written and handed in a long time ago."

Joan's gaze met hers. "I wish I had now."

"So do I. I'm afraid we're too late to sign up for Yellowstone now."

"Don't be such a pessimist," Joan said airily.

They hurried downstairs but were just in time to see the office door close.

Joan stopped, her attractive face clouding.

"They can't do this to us."

"Maybe not, but they just did."

It was after lunch before they were able to get into the office to see about jobs for the summer. Miss Hendricks, who was taking care of the applications for the school, looked up.

"And I suppose you want to go to Yellowstone too?" she asked.

"How did you guess?" Joan wanted to know.

"Yellowstone seems to be all the rage this year. Everybody's been wanting to sign up to work there."

"Then there are still some openings?" Felicia asked.

The smile left Miss Hendricks' usually pleasant face.

"I'm sorry. The park only asked us for a certain number of girls. Our quota was filled before classes this morning."

Joan groaned her disappointment.

"Thank you," Felicia said. She touched her friend's arm and would have turned to leave, but Miss Hendricks stopped them.

"Don't you girls want to sign up for something else?" she asked.

The girls glanced at each other questioningly.

"We'll go over the list again and see if anything looks good to us," Joan told her.

"I do have a suggestion for you. A request for two girls came in just this morning." She picked up an envelope from her desk. "I haven't gotten it on the board yet, and I don't think it will be open for long after it's posted."

Felicia asked about it.

"Sit down, and I'll read you the letter." Miss Hendricks continued to talk as she took the stationery from the envelope. "Mr. Rutledge and his wife have been running a resort in the Black Hills of South Dakota for a number of years."

At the mention of the location, Joan's nose wrinkled distastefully.

Miss Hendricks saw it and stiffened.

"Really, Miss Bailey. I'm only trying to be helpful."

"I'm sorry," Joan replied, "but South Dakota and the Black Hills sound like such dreary places."

"Have you ever been there?"

"No, but it sounds like a drag."

"You shouldn't criticize a place until you know what it is like. I've spent some time in the Black Hills on a number of occasions and have found them charming."

"What is the job like?" Felicia broke in.

"I want to tell you about the Rutledges first. They had no time for Christ until a few months ago when they wandered into a little church in Rapid City, and for the first time, they learned that Jesus Christ had a claim on their lives." She glanced over the letter. "I won't read all of this. It would take too long. It just tells how they called the pastor a week later and drove all the way down to talk to him about their own need for a personal relationship with Christ. Now that they're Christians, they would like to see that their resort is a testimony to those who come there."

"I see," Felicia said. That did make the Rutledge jobs sound attractive. They hadn't even considered the possibility of getting work in a Christian place. "What would we be doing?"

"They want two Christian girls to look after the children of guests for regular periods each day, girls who would be capable of giving an hour's Bible study each morning or afternoon."

"That sounds like fun," Felicia said immediately.

But Joan wasn't so sure. "It would be all right for a while, but I don't know whether I'd want to take a job where I'd be taking care of kids all the time."

There was a brief pause.

Miss Hendricks frowned thoughtfully.

"I would like to see you girls take this job," she said. "I'm sure you would be able to do a good job for the Rutledges, and I think the work would be good for you. It's irregular, but if you think you're interested, I will wait until morning to contact them."

"Thank you," Felicia said earnestly. It was obvious that she had already made up her own mind. At least, that was the conclusion Joan reached. Sighing, she turned back to the desk.

"You'd just as well put our names down now." Her resignation was evident. "Felicia's already got her mind made up that we're going there, and she'll never leave me alone until I agree. I'd just as well do it now."

Felicia wrinkled her nose at her, but she was smiling as Miss Hendricks wrote down their names and gave them application blanks to fill out.

"I just know we're going to love it at the Rutledge Mountain Resort, Joan," she said as they left the office and started up to their rooms on the second floor.

"Don't be too sure of that."

CHAPTER 3

RUTLEDGE MOUNTAIN RESORT

Felicia and Joan had a short week at home with their families before going out to the Black Hills of South Dakota to the Rutledge Mountain Resort where they were to work for the summer. They flew to Rapid City and took the bus to Silver City, a little town in the valley at the foot of the mountain where Mr. and Mrs. Rutledge had their resort.

Anita Rutledge drove down to meet them. She was a willowy natural blonde who looked at least ten years younger than she actually was, a tall, attractive woman who would have been as comfortable and at ease in an evening gown as in the slacks she was wearing.

"You must be Felicia and Joan!" she exclaimed, approaching them with her hands extended in greeting. "I had you picked out when I came around the corner and saw you standing there. I'm sorry I'm late, but this has been one of *those* days."

They got their bags and went to the car with her. She was chattering amiably.

"I'm so glad we were able to get Christian girls for this job." Her smile was warm and pleasant. "You see, Clark and I haven't been saved very long; but after we decided to walk with Christ, we decided that we wanted to make our resort speak for Him too. That was when we decided to use Christian girls to take care of the children of our guests."

She turned off the main road at a newly painted arrow that pointed up the trail to the Rutledge Mountain Resort.

"But we got the idea of using Christians so late that we were afraid we wouldn't be able to find girls to help us," she went on. "Then we got your applications. I don't mind telling you that both Clark and I looked on them as an answer to our prayers."

"And we felt the same way," Felicia said.

Joan nodded.

"After we thought it over, that is. At first, we didn't know whether we wanted to spend the summer taking care of somebody else's kids or not."

"I know just how you felt," Anita Rutledge replied with surprising candor. "I think I'd have had the same reservations at your age. But it's really not as bad as it sounds."

She went on to give them a rundown on their responsibilities.

"The parents will take their children to breakfast, so you won't get them before 9:00 or 9:30 except on those rare occasions when their moms and dads go on an early trail ride or up the mountain, fishing."

"That doesn't sound so bad," Joan agreed.

"You'll have them through the noon hour in the dining room, but they are supposed to rest between 1:00 and 2:00 so you'll get a little break for that hour. You'll be responsible for them from 2:00 until 6:00. The evenings they will spend with their parents."

"I told you that you didn't have to worry about working nights," Felicia said, her eyes twinkling. "You'll have your evenings free."

"So will you," Joan murmured good naturedly, "but that probably won't do either of us a lot of good. I suppose every guy on the place is either married or spoken for or is too old or too young."

There was mystery in Anita Rutledge's laughter.

"Don't be too sure of that."

Felicia turned to face her friend. "Did you hear that? Maybe you won't be so sorry that we didn't get to go to Yellowstone Park to work after all."

Joan flushed. "Do you have to tell everything you know?"

The lane to the resort was long and twisting, pressed in on either side by pine trees that threatened to choke it out of existence. So close were the trees above the lane that only a thin ribbon of blue sky was visible. The hush was electric. Even the birds and the squirrels seemed to respect the serene quiet of the lane and made no sound.

The occupants of the car fell silent. Joan moistened her lips with the tip of her tongue after a moment or two but did not speak.

At last, they rounded a bend and burst into a small clearing. Beyond it, in a cluster of trees, stood the main lodge. Scattered with well-planned abandon around the spacious grass-carpeted grounds was a series of individual log cabins connected to each other and the main lodge by a spidery network of trails. On the opposite side was the horse barn.

Felicia gasped when she saw the sparkling little lake down the slope a few brief steps from the lodge.

"It's lovely!" she whispered.

"It is, isn't it? You know, it affects almost everyone who sees it for the first time. In fact, it still affects me that way, and I don't know how many hundreds of times I've seen it as I leave the lane. Silver Lake is one of the charms of our little place."

Joan drew in her breath deeply.

"Now I am *really* glad we came here to work! I've never seen a spot half so beautiful."

The car came to a stop near the lodge, and Felicia reached to open the door so she and Joan could get out. Before they could do so, however, two boys about their age or a year older disengaged themselves from the shadows and came out to the vehicle that had just arrived.

"Hello, Mrs. Rutledge," they said. Although they were talking to Anita, they were looking at Joan and Felicia.

"Anything we can carry for you?" one of them asked.

"You'll have to ask these two young ladies." Mrs. Rutledge jumped lightly from the car and whisked to the rear. "But I'm sure they would like to have help with their luggage."

One of the boys opened the back of the car.

"Come on, Phil," he called to his companion. "Give me a hand."

At the mention of the boy's name, Mrs. Rutledge stopped what she was doing and glanced back at the girls who were just getting out of the car.

"Oh, my goodness!" she exclaimed. "I completely forgot to introduce you. What are you going to think of me? First, I'm late to pick you up, and now I don't introduce you to the two eligible young men on the staff."

Felicia and Joan both colored delicately, but Mrs. Rutledge seemed unaware that what she had said embarrassed them slightly.

"This is Ted Beck, and this is Phil Wallace," she went on, the words gushing out. "We got them from one of the Bible schools in Colorado. They double as lifeguards at the pool and take some of the older boys on trail rides and teach them mountain climbing."

Neither Felicia nor Joan heard what the wife of their summer employer said next. They were watching in silence while Ted and Phil got their suitcases from the back of the car.

Ted was as stocky as Phil was lank, a broad-chested young man already bronzed by the summer sun. His smile was quick, and most of the time, his eyes were laughing.

Phil Wallace was more serious, a spindling bamboo-fishing pole of a guy who would probably make a basketball coach drool over the prospect of having such a player to snag rebounds and make jump shots.

Anita Rutledge rushed toward the lodge, flinging some sort of excuse about having forgotten to do something over her shoulder. At the door, she turned and came back.

"Put the girls in Room 22, Ted," she instructed. "The guests in that room checked out this morning."

The boys carried their suitcases to the room Mrs. Rutledge sent them to. On the way, they asked Felicia and Joan about the school they were going to and how they came to be at the Rutledge resort that summer.

"I guess it's about the same for us," Phil said when they told them. "We were planning to help with some missionary building in Alaska this summer, but things didn't work out."

"Actually," Ted added, "we didn't know what we were going to do until we got the chance to come here."

Room 22 wasn't the sort of room Felicia and Joan figured the Rutledges would use for those who worked for them. It was almost twice as large as the one they shared at Wellington and had a huge picture window overlooking the pool and Silver Lake.

"If you want to see me," Ted told Felicia, "all you have to do is go to the window and look right over there. I'll be guarding the lives of the swimmers."

Roses bloomed in her cheeks as Joan snickered.

Phil looked at his watch. "If you don't want to get us both in trouble with Mr. Rutledge, you'd better can the chatter so we can get back to work. We've got plenty to do."

"You go ahead. I'll catch up with you."

"Nothing doing. You'll come with me right now."

"Okay, okay. If that's the way it's got to be." He turned back to Felicia. "He tells people his name is Phil Wallace, but it's really Simon Legree. And I'm the slave he keeps whipping to get more work done."

"You look abused," Felicia said, laughing.

"I am, dear lady. I am."

"Come on, Romeo! Back to the coal mine."

"See? This is the way it is all the time."

They went down the hall together, still ragging each other good-naturedly.

Slowly, Joan turned to Felicia, accusation coloring her voice. "And *you* were the one who kept teasing me about wanting to go to Yellowstone Park where the boys are!"

"I couldn't help *that,* now could I?"

"I didn't see you trying very hard."

A smile tugged the corner of Felicia's mouth upward.

"He is sort of cute, isn't he?"

Joan grinned.

"And so's Phil Wallace. It looks to me as though it's going to be a most interesting summer."

"We came out here to take care of the guests' children. Remember?"

"Me, remember? Look who's talking."

They unpacked their suitcases and hung their clothes in the closet.

CHAPTER 4

"GOD DOESN'T LOVE ME!"

The following morning, Felicia and Joan met the youngsters they would be taking care of. There were fourteen boys and girls from six to twelve years old in the first group. Most of them had arrived only hours before and didn't know anyone else. They stood around awkwardly, wondering if they were going to like these two strange young ladies who were going to be in charge of them and if they were going to have any fun.

Joan sensed the situation as she called them to attention briefly.

"We don't know any of you," she began, "and you don't know us. So, what do you say that we spend the first few minutes getting acquainted?"

She introduced herself and Felicia to them and asked each his name. Felicia noted them mentally – or tried to. It would be hard getting to know them by name at first, but after a time, both she and Joan would know each of them by name.

Joan had everyone laughing by the time she turned them over to Felicia.

"I'm going to tell you something about the things we will be doing while you're here," Felicia said, lowering her voice mysteriously. They grew quiet in order to hear her better. "We're going to do some mountain climbing and have picnics and trail rides and nature hikes. There'll be a craft to do and a time to swim each day."

"Great!" one bright-eyed lad piped.

"You can tell your moms and dads about most of the things we're going to be doing." She was scarcely speaking above a whisper, and they leaned forward intently to catch every word. "But we are going to have some surprises too. And we're supposed to keep very quiet about them. No one is supposed to tell *anyone* about our plans. It will spoil everything if they find out our secrets."

Fourteen pairs of eyes were fixed tensely on her as she went on to describe what they were planning to do. Afterward, several came up to talk with them about the plans, talking in whispers themselves.

The kids liked Joan and Felicia from the first day and were eager to please them. They found the time of Bible stories especially intriguing. Some of them acted as though they had never heard the simple stories of the Bible before and were anxious for the storytime to come. There were no special discipline problems the first week, and the girls felt that the summer was going to be a success.

Then Mitzi Simmons came to the resort with her father, John. Anita Rutledge found Joan and Felicia in the dining hall the evening Mitzi arrived and told them about her.

"I thought I had better tell you about her before I forget it, but her father says she isn't feeling too well now. It may be tomorrow before she joins your group."

"Oh, that's too bad," Felicia said, her concern showing in her eyes. "Do you suppose we ought to go and see her?"

Mrs. Rutledge frowned.

"I'm not so sure whether that would be wise or not. It's rather an unusual situation, Felicia. Why don't you wait until she joins your group? Then, if you want to go and visit her and you feel that it's the thing to do it, it would be fine."

When Mrs. Rutledge was gone, Felicia turned to Joan.

"She didn't even tell us the girl's name."

"That's right." Her best friend laughed musically. "But that's about par for Mrs. Rutledge. She's one of the sweetest persons in the world, but she hardly ever remembers everything that she's supposed to do."

But at the moment, Felicia wasn't thinking about Anita Rutledge alone. She was wondering why she didn't want them to go and visit this new little girl who was sick. It didn't add up.

She voiced her opinion to Joan.

"It doesn't seem right to me either. And it isn't like Mrs. Rutledge. She's a kind person."

They were so very busy, however, that they completely forgot the incident. And, the day of the nature hike, one of the mothers came over to talk with Felicia and Joan as they were about to call their group to order. The woman only wanted to thank them for watching over her young son. It took so long, however, that the kids grew restless and were anxious to be gone. The two young leaders scarcely noticed the new girl who was with them for the first time.

It was not until the kids began to collect their specimens and Felicia went over to talk to Mitzi that they knew who she was.

"I'm beginning to understand a little of what Mrs. Rutledge meant when she said what she did about Mitzi Simmons," Felicia said when she and Joan were away from their youthful charges. "She's one of the strangest girls that I have ever been around."

Joan's head bobbed, almost imperceptibly, in agreement. "In a way, she acts shy, but I get the feeling that it's more than that."

"So do I."

Joan shrugged the problem away, at least for the moment. "Maybe when she gets to know us a little better, she'll enter into things."

The following day, it rained, so they were unable to have the wiener roast down by the lake as they had planned. Instead, they postponed it until the following day and switched to some indoor games.

At first, Mitzi refused to take part at all, but at Joan's urging, she finally agreed to enter in. The other kids squealed with glee as their side surged ahead but not Mitzi. She acted as though she didn't care who won or if anybody did. And when her team was victorious, she didn't even smile, although her teammates were chattering excitedly. It wasn't long until the other kids noticed it.

"Look at that grump over there," the nine-year-old who brought the garter snake to Felicia said, jerking his head in Mitzi's direction. "I don't know why she didn't stay back at the lodge where she belongs. She never wants to do anything the rest of us want to."

"Now, Donald," Felicia protested sternly. "We don't talk about others that way."

"Well, she is. She's just an old grouch who doesn't try to win. I sure don't want her on my team again."

"I don't want you to say any more about Mitzi," Felicia repeated, her voice growing even more stern. "Or you may find yourself sitting out a couple of games."

"Aw–" But he said no more.

Felicia watched Mitzi with the others the next two or three days, hoping that Joan was right in saying she would become more friendly and cooperative as she got better acquainted. However, there was little change in her. She either took no part at all or was so passive and indifferent that the others were infuriated with her. She didn't even get excited when they were finally able to have the wiener roast down by the lake.

After they had finished gorging themselves on hot dogs and roasted marshmallows, Felicia got them seated cross-legged on the rock ledge near the water. Joan began to teach a short lesson on the love of God.

"God loves us so much," she said, "that He sent His only Son to die on the cross so that you and I might go to heaven." She went on to talk about the love God has for everybody, telling them that it was His love for them that caused Him to send Jesus to die on the cross. She paused and picked up a picture that went along with the story.

"God loves everybody," she repeated.

"God doesn't love *me!*" The words exploded venomously from Mitzi Simmons' lips.

Heads jerked in her direction. Everyone was staring at her in shock and disbelief.

She hadn't intended to speak out. As she saw that everyone was looking at her, the color drained from her cheeks, and her lips began to tremble.

Joan Bailey was so stunned by the sudden outburst that, momentarily, she had no answer for the distraught girl.

"I–" The words clung to the roof of her mouth.

Mitzi got to her feet.

"God might like the rest of you," she blurted, "but He doesn't love me! And He never has!" With that, she spun on her heel and dashed into the forest that crowded close against the beach.

The lesson was forgotten as everyone stared into the woods where Mitzi had disappeared. Joan looked helplessly at Felicia, as though she was asking her what she should do next.

"Why don't you go on with the rest of the lesson, Joan?" she suggested calmly. "I'll go and talk with Mitzi."

Joan did as Felicia suggested and finished the story, but she could just as well have stopped. After Mitzi Simmons' sudden outburst and dash away from the group, nobody was listening to anything that Joan said.

Felicia wasn't sure just where Mitzi had gone or where she would find her. A prayer welled in her heart as she moved forward, a prayer that she would find Mitzi and that the distraught girl would listen to her.

She found her a few moments later, standing beside a thick clump of brush, head down and her small hands clenched.

"Mitzi," Felicia said softly as she came up behind the girl.

No answer.

"Mitzi." She put a hand on her frail shoulder. "I'm terribly sorry that you feel God doesn't love you. It means that Joan and I have failed in our efforts to tell you about God."

Mitzi stiffened.

"God doesn't love me! If He did, He wouldn't let things happen the way they are!" Her voice broke.

Felicia realized that this was not the time for talking. She wrapped an arm tenderly around Mitzi and drew her close, asking God quietly for guidance and strength as she tried to talk to the sad little girl.

After a time, Mitzi began to quiet. Only then did Felicia begin to talk about it.

"Would you like to tell me why you don't think that God loves you?" she asked.

The girl shook her head, fighting violently to keep back the tears.

"Is there any way that I could help?"

"There's nothing anybody can do, Miss Cartright!" She started to cry again, softly.

Felicia gathered her into her arms and held her. She didn't speak. There was nothing she could say. All she could do was to show Mitzi that she cared – that she truly loved her and wanted to help her.

CHAPTER 5

KIDS' NIGHT

It was only with considerable difficulty that Felicia was able to get Mitzi to rejoin the others.

"They'll all laugh at me if I do," she protested. "They'll make fun of me because of what I did."

"No, they won't. No one will say a word."

"You don't know."

"I certainly do." She wouldn't let them say anything that would hurt Mitzi more than she was hurt already.

"All right," the girl promised, "but if anyone says anything to me, I'm going to leave this stupid old place and never come back!"

No one said anything to Mitzi. It might have been better if they had. But nobody said anything at all to her. They acted as though she wasn't even there. Her temper bristled, and defiance glittered darkly in her eyes.

Both Felicia and Joan were upset by the way Mitzi had exploded and the reaction of the other kids to her.

"I don't know what it is about her that bothers me, Joan," Felicia said, "but there's something wrong in her life. Something terribly wrong."

"You aren't telling me anything. She's an explosion waiting to happen if I ever saw one."

"I don't think I've ever seen any child as unhappy as she appears to be."

"The question is," Joan said, "what are we going to do about it?"

Felicia sighed. "I wish I knew."

Before dinner that evening, they sought out Mr. Rutledge and told him what had taken place.

"She acted so strangely," Felicia concluded, "that we thought maybe we should come to you and see if her dad told you anything that would lead you to believe that she is disturbed emotionally."

Clark Rutledge shook his head.

"No, he didn't. As a matter of fact, he didn't tell me anything about his daughter, except that he thought her mother might be coming up later if she could get away."

The girls thanked him and moved in the direction of the dining room.

"Mr. Rutledge didn't act as though he was very concerned about Mitzi, did he?" Joan said.

"I think he had the idea that we were exaggerating her problems."

They paused in the dining room doorway looking over the small group that had arrived to eat. It was still early, and only a few of the guests had come in.

"There's Mr. Simmons, Joan," Felicia said. "Let's go over and talk to him."

She started in the direction of the tall, sandy-haired individual who was seated alone near the window. Joan followed.

They introduced themselves and told him what they did at the resort.

"We have Mitzi in our group," Joan said.

"Oh, yes." The lines about his eyes deepened somberly. "Won't you sit down. I've been sitting here wishing that I could have the chance to talk to you."

He spooned sugar into his coffee and stirred it carefully while Felicia and Joan eyed him curiously.

"When Mitzi came in a little while ago, she was all upset. As a matter of fact, she looked as though she had been crying."

Felicia nodded. "She had been."

"I wanted her to come in and have something to eat with me, but she didn't want to. She said she had a headache and felt like going to sleep." He leaned forward slightly, and a new earnestness tinged his voice. "I don't mind telling you that it bothers me to have her so upset."

One of the waitresses came, and the girls placed their orders. While they were waiting to be served, they told him what had taken place.

"I'm relieved to know that was what was bothering her."

"It's more than that," Joan said.

"That's right," Felicia added seriously. "Ever since she came here, she's acted so very unhappy. I can't help wondering what it is that makes her think God doesn't love her."

John Simmons' eyes narrowed.

"To be honest with you, I can't say that I blame Mitzi," he retorted coldly. "He's never done anything for me. I can tell you that much."

The girls must have stared at him, their surprise and concern showing.

"Don't be so shocked," he told them. "I'm not a bank robber or a murderer, and I don't kidnap little kids. It's just that I feel the same way Mitzi does about the love of God. It might exist, but I'll be frank. I've never seen any evidence of it."

He seemed embarrassed by the fact that he had revealed so much of his own personal feelings. He changed the subject quickly and refused to let it come back to his daughter. When Felicia or Joan tried to talk about her, he parried their questions or broke in with something far different.

He finished eating as quickly as he could, took a final sip of coffee, and put his napkin on the table beside his plate.

"If you girls will excuse me, I'd better go up and see how she's doing." He got to his feet and started away.

He was almost at the door when he stopped and came back apologetically.

"I'm sorry I was so rude as to leave the way I did, but I'm most concerned about Mitzi."

"That's all right," they told him. "We're concerned about her too."

"I know you are. And I deeply appreciate it. I know you have her best interests at heart."

They mumbled something or other in reply and watched as he walked away.

It was two or three minutes before either of them could speak. At last, Joan found voice.

"He seems as bitter as Mitzi is," she said softly. "Somehow, I didn't expect that. I–I" Her voice trailed away into a tense, expectant hush.

Felicia was toying with her iced tea thoughtfully but without realizing what she was doing.

"You know, Joan," she said, "we spent at least half an hour talking with him, but he really didn't tell us anything about either Mitzi or himself."

"I didn't realize that, but it's true." The corners of Joan's mouth tightened. "Why do you suppose he's so bitter about God? He's worse than Mitzi was."

Felicia nodded her agreement. Mr. Simmons did act as though he had a personal quarrel with God.

Phil and Ted came up just then.

"We saw you," Ted exclaimed, pulling out a chair and sitting down. "Didn't anyone ever tell you that the hired help isn't supposed to mingle with the paying guests? Wherever are your good manners?"

"We had a problem," Felicia told him.

"And he has an advice-to-the-lovelorn column. Is that it?"

"To tell you the truth, we were talking to him about his daughter, Mitzi."

"She's that Simmons kid, isn't she?" Phil asked, pulling out a chair across from his pal and sitting down.

"I've noticed her at the swimming pool," Ted put in. "She acts as though she doesn't have a friend or an interest in the world."

"And that's not all." Felicia told them about the outburst of the afternoon. Both boys were very interested in what Mitzi had done. They discussed the matter with them thoroughly, asked a few questions, and before Felicia and Joan left, they volunteered to pray for Mitzi and her father.

"We can't do anything about bitterness like that," Ted told them. "Only God can straighten them out in their thinking. But we will talk to Him about them."

The following day, Mitzi Simmons was with the other kids just as though nothing had ever happened. Her face was still taut, and defiance still gleamed in her eyes, but she was there, the same as she had been before.

Felicia tried hard to be friendly to her, but Mitzi

did not respond. It was almost as though she lacked the feelings that other people possessed.

The next few days were repetitions of the days that had gone before. Felicia and Joan worked with their young charges in handcrafts, nature study, and games, and on one or two occasions, took them on short trail rides. For an hour each day, they sang choruses, learned Bible verses, and had simple Bible stories or lessons.

Felicia and Joan had said little about the approaching Kids' Night since the first time they went on a nature hike to collect specimens, but the excitement about it seemed to capture everybody. Even before the kids had finished anything in handcraft to be shown to their moms and dads, they were talking with each other about it.

"You know," someone said, "I heard Miss Joan and Mrs. Rutledge talking about it. We're going to get to introduce our parents to everybody, and we get to show them our nature displays and our swimming badges and what we've made in handcraft."

One of the girls nodded.

"And maybe we'll get to sing choruses and say the Bible verses we have learned." She was the one who had mastered more verses than anyone else.

Mitzi's lips tightened. She looked up at Felicia, desperation kindling in her eyes. Then she looked quickly away.

The Kids' Night seemed to sneak up on them. One

day they announced it, and the days that followed rushed by so rapidly they were gone, and Kids' Night was upon them.

Some of the youngsters had to rush frantically to get their handwork finished in time. But, when the big night arrived, everything was in order. Each of the boys and girls in Felicia and Joan's care was present with his parents when Joan got to her feet to introduce Donald Brentwood, the sharp little nine-year-old who had brought Felicia the snake. Proudly, he told everybody the names of his parents, asked them to stand, and showed them the leather work he had just finished a few minutes before.

A boy and two girls followed. Then it was Mitzi's turn.

"And now we will have Mitzi Simmons come forward."

All was silent.

"Mitzi." Joan spoke louder.

Somebody from the back row spoke up. "Mitzi Simmons and her dad left a minute ago!"

Felicia and Joan glanced at each other significantly. They hadn't expected that development, but they were not surprised.

The program had to go on, but as far as they were concerned, the interest had died. When the last youngster had taken part, both Joan and Felicia felt that the program had been a miserable failure.

CHAPTER 6

A SUDDEN STORM

Felicia and Joan were busy on the lakeshore for some time after the guests went back to their rooms. They had to pack what was left of the food and make sure that the fire was out. It was half an hour later before they were ready to leave.

"I feel a little sick inside when I think about Mitzi," Felicia said, staring back to the lodge. "Why do you suppose she and her father left before she had her turn on the program?"

Joan shrugged. "At first, I figured we might be able to help her, but now I wonder. I've never seen anyone quite so difficult."

Felicia paused, staring off into the darkness. She wasn't ready to say that nothing could be done for Mitzi. One look in those somber eyes made her realize how desperately the girl needed help; but Mitzi was so distant, so remote and unreachable.

The next morning, the others had all gathered and were playing games, but there was no sign of Mitzi. Felicia and Joan were beginning to think she wasn't going to come at all when the side door of the lodge opened, and she came shuffling out to join them. She approached reluctantly, as though each step was an effort. Her head was down, hiding the hurt in her limpid eyes.

"Hello." Joan went over to her.

She answered shortly.

"I'm so glad you came this morning. I was beginning to think you were sick. Especially when you left the program last night before it was over."

Mitzi looked up, eyes dark and forbidding.

"Dad and I decided not to stay," she muttered decisively.

"But you worked so hard on the moccasins you were going to show." Joan's voice softened almost to a whisper. "I thought yours was the best pair of all."

For a brief instant, pride gleamed in the girl's eyes. Then something akin to anger drove the pride away.

"Dad doesn't care about any dumb old moccasins," she blurted defiantly. "Neither do I. It's stupid making all that junk!"

"I don't think it's stupid at all," Joan countered. "You should have heard what everyone was saying about all the nice things that were shown."

Tears sparkled in Mitzi's eyes.

"I don't care!" She turned her back on Joan and stalked away angrily.

During the next few days, Felicia and Joan tried to cultivate Mitzi's friendship, to gain her confidence so she would talk to them. But it seemed useless. She would answer when they talked to her but that was all. She was even less cooperative than she had been before the Kids' Night program.

"She's built a cocoon around herself," Joan observed, "and I don't have the slightest clue as to how to get through it."

"We've got to find out what's bugging her, for one thing. She acts to me as though she's carrying the whole world on her shoulders."

"And how are we going to find out what's bugging her?" Joan asked. "She won't say anything, and her dad claims he doesn't know. We're at a dead end."

Felicia's lips tightened to a thin, hard line.

"There's got to be some way of getting her to open up."

"If there is, we sure haven't been able to find it." Joan went to the closet and hung up her jacket. "It's like you used to tell me, Felicia. The real problem is spiritual. If we could get her to see the need for letting God have control of her life, she'd be well on the way to getting straightened out."

Felicia agreed with her. "But the big problem is going to be to get Mitzi to see it. We've both tried to talk to her about her relationship with Christ, but it hasn't done any good."

"I know. I tried to talk with her again yesterday, but she wouldn't listen."

During the next several days, Mitzi's rebellion seemed to grow. From the first, she had been reluctant to take part in the activities Felicia and Joan planned. Now, however, she was openly hostile. She would stand to one side, disapproval glittering in her eyes.

"Me play that stupid old game?" Derision toned her laughter. "If I couldn't find anything better to do than that, I think I'd quit."

In spite of her concern for Mitzi, Joan's temper surged. "You don't have to stay out here if you think everything we do is too childish for you, Mitzi," she reminded her. "I'm sure Mr. Rutledge wouldn't mind if you go back to the lodge."

The girl's lips quivered. "Maybe Mr. Rutledge wouldn't care, but Dad would! I'd rather be with him, but he says I've got to come out here with the other kids! And I hate it!"

She turned her back on Joan abruptly, her frail shoulders trembling. But there were no tears. Mitzi saw to that.

Felicia and Joan found themselves thinking first about Mitzi and what she liked as they planned the activities for the kids in their care. Thinking back, they recalled that she seemed to enjoy the trail ride more than anything else. So they planned another.

That proved to be most popular with the rest of the kids too. Several squealed with delight when the announcement was made. Even Mitzi smiled broadly.

Joan glanced at Felicia and winked.

"We've finally done it!" Felicia exclaimed in guarded tones to her best friend. "We've found something that interests Mitzi."

"You hope," Joan said. "We can't be sure of anything when it comes to her."

"Pessimist."

"Realist is a better word. I hope you're right, Felicia, but I won't believe it with Mitzi until I see it. She's fooled us before."

The next morning, huge white powder puffs drifted aimlessly about the sky, cutting the blue into intricate, ever-changing patterns. It was a breathless day on the mountain slope, although the wind was shoving the clouds around at higher altitudes, the sort of day when even the aspen slept.

Phil and Ted came down to help saddle the horses.

"Figuring on a trail ride this morning?" Phil asked, glancing up.

"Shouldn't we?" Joan asked.

"It looks a bit like rain to me." He threw the stirrup over the saddle horn so it was out of the way and drew up the cinch to the third hole in the heavy strap. "But then, it looked like rain yesterday, too, and there wasn't any. It probably won't rain today either."

Joan swung into the saddle. "I guess getting wet

is the worst that could happen to us, even if it should rain."

Phil held her mount's bridle momentarily.

"Don't be too sure of that. There are some sizable cliffs around here and some narrow trails that can get slick and treacherous. If it does rain, be careful."

Joan heard a slight sound to her right, and her head jerked in that direction. There was Mitzi, listening intently. Her face was white and drawn and her gaze shifty.

She had heard what Phil said!

For an instant, Joan was furious at the tall young man who was standing beside her horse.

But then, she reasoned, he didn't know how things were with Mitzi. Not everything, that was. And he was only concerned about their safety. She was sorry she had lost her temper and was glad that she had said nothing to him.

Yet, as far as Mitzi Simmons was concerned, the damage had been done. Anticipation, never very high, died in her eyes, and every now and then, she glanced upward at the sky. The others laughed as they rode or looked around, enjoying the slowly unfolding scene around them.

Not Mitzi.

She alternately stared at her saddle horn and at the moving clouds above them. It was fortunate for her that her mount was well trained for the trail. He followed the horse ahead of him without direction from his rider.

They left the resort by way of the lane, took a trail up the mountain for half a mile or so, and angled toward the spot near the sheer rock cliff where they could look down on the resort road to the highway and beyond to the village of Silver City.

They had traveled a mile or two, and Joan had all but forgotten Phil's warning when, suddenly, they were lashed with rain. Although Phil had predicted its coming, it was one of those sudden storms that sneaks in over the trees as silently as an eagle gliding in its search for food.

One moment it was not. The next it was, ripping violently across the helpless mountain slope, lashing it with rain and wind. In the first sudden torrent, they were all soaked to the skin. In the same instant, the wind swept through the trees with a force that bent down branches as big around as a man's leg.

Lightning split the sky, slashing down from dark clouds to drive into the ground, quivering before it vanished. Seconds later, the sharp blast of thunder and deepening roll gave voice to the vivid flash of light.

The storm descended so swiftly that it immobilized the little group on horseback for one long, terrifying instant. One of the girls, a bit younger than the rest, began to cry almost hysterically.

Felicia took charge with a calmness that quieted even the most uneasy.

"Now listen, everybody!" Her voice sounded above the rumble of thunder and the coughing wind. "Get hold of yourselves! All of you! That isn't going to help any!"

"But I'm scared!" a younger girl protested, shivering.

"So am I."

"And cold!"

They were all huddled as closely together as they could be on horseback, hunching against the wind.

CHAPTER 7

SOMEONE WHO CAN HELP

Joan kicked her mount in the flanks and rode over to Felicia. The kids were all around them, but she spoke guardedly so they wouldn't be overheard.

"What are we going to do?"

"I don't know, but we've got to get out of this storm. That's for sure."

Joan hesitated momentarily.

"Didn't we pass a cave out this way the last time we were here?" she asked.

Once Joan mentioned the cave, Felicia remembered it. It was a quarter of a mile or so ahead, only a few hundred yards from the place where the trail dwindled to uselessness on a sheer granite cliff. They had gone by it the week before.

"Listen to me!" Felicia raised her voice against the howl of the storm. "We're going to ride ahead to a cave a quarter of a mile up the trail!"

Even as she finished, two or three of the older boys eased forward on the reins and would have kicked their horses to a gallop had Felicia not stopped them.

"Wait a minute! Wait a minute! We're all going together!"

There was some grumbling, but the girls held a firm hand and got the wet, miserable little group started up the trail in single file.

It was only a short ride to the cave where Felicia and Joan had them dismount and tie their horses to nearby trees.

"You bigger boys!" Felicia ordered. "Tie the horses of the smaller ones!"

In a minute or two everyone was inside the cave, shivering, wet, and cold.

"Now," Joan said, "to get a fire built."

"You can't start a fire with wet wood," a scoffing twelve-year-old informed her.

Joan laughed good-naturedly. "You just watch us."

She and Felicia went out into the driving rain to get wood. Instead of taking branches from the ground, however, they broke the dead branches off the trees near the mouth of the cave. In a few minutes, they were back, their arms loaded with wood.

"I still say you can't start a fire with wet wood."

"Have you got a knife?" Joan asked him.

He handed her his jackknife and watched, still disbelieving, as she selected a pine branch a little larger than her thumb and began to make shavings. With those in the center, she made a small teepee of twigs.

"It's not going to burn," he muttered under his breath.

Joan touched a match to it. It sputtered briefly, and a thin yellow tongue began to lick upward toward the twigs. In a few minutes, the fire was burning steadily and the youngsters crowded around to soak up its warmth.

"You can't build a fire with wet wood," the boy was muttering to himself. "You can't do it."

"That's right," Joan told him. "The secret is to find wood that isn't wet." She told him that she had taken branches off the standing trees to use as kindling. "So, the only water they have on them is on the outside. Actually, it's quite dry in spite of the rain. Wood on the ground soaks up moisture and can be wet all the way through and almost impossible to use for a fire."

He stared at her in disbelief.

"How'd you know that?" he demanded. "You're just a girl!"

"Can't a girl know anything about the woods?" she asked.

Joan had built the fire in the mouth of the large cave and kept the size small enough so there was a minimum of smoke. But it was large enough to spread its warmth to the little group of youngsters.

It wasn't long until they were all feeling better and started to sing.

At first, they sang fun songs, but after a few minutes, Felicia suggested a chorus. After that, the kids did the same. They sang lustily and with more fervor than they had ever shown before. They were all enjoying themselves so much that nobody noticed that Mitzi wasn't with the others until she coughed.

Felicia turned and saw her sitting near the mouth of the cave. She got to her feet and went over to her.

"Mitzi," she said softly.

The girl did not look up. "Just leave me alone!" She was near tears.

Felicia ignored her bitter demand.

"It's much warmer over by the fire than it is here."

"I don't care." She drew away slightly, as though to show that she wanted to be alone.

Felicia sat down beside her, and for the space of two or three minutes, neither spoke.

"What is troubling you, Mitzi?" she asked at last, a new gentleness in her voice.

The girl looked up, her irritation showing in her eyes.

"There's nothing wrong, except that I want to be alone! Is that such a terrible sin?"

Felicia studied her somber young face intently.

Nothing she could say at the moment would help Mitzi. Or so it seemed. Yet she could not leave her alone. She sat with her in silence, sharing the girl's turbulence and heartache by her presence if nothing else.

They were both so intent in their thoughts that they hadn't even noticed that the rain was letting up until Joan called to them.

"We'd better go before it starts to rain again."

Felicia stood and was about to tell Mitzi they had to leave when she changed her mind.

"You go ahead, Joan. Mitzi and I will be along in a little while."

Her best friend nodded significantly to indicate that she understood.

She sat down near the distraught girl patiently. Mitzi raised her head.

"You don't have to stay with me," she retorted, a defiant tone creeping into her voice. "I can look after myself. I don't need you or anyone else!"

"I wanted to stay here with you," Felicia told her.

The pause was long and weighted. At last, the girl spoke reluctantly, as though she didn't want to but could not keep back the word.

"Why?"

"Because I want to be with you when you're so unhappy, Mitzi. I know there's nothing I can do to make you feel any better, but I do want you to know that I care about you."

Mitzi's throat choked, and it was all she could do to keep from crying.

After a time, Felicia continued slowly. "It is true that there's nothing I can do to make you feel better.

I'm as helpless as you are when it comes to that. But I know Someone who can help."

The girl looked up, defiance straightening her mouth and smoldering in her eyes.

"No, you don't!" she retorted. "Nobody can help me!"

Felicia's smile was warm and compassionate, like the early spring sunshine on a flower bed.

"I used to feel the same as you do now when I was your age or a little older. Then I found that there was Someone who could help me. I learned that if I was a follower of Jesus, He would help me with all my problems."

Mitzi still did not reply, yet she watched Felicia intently, waiting for her to go on.

"Jesus wants to help you, my dear, but He won't force Himself on you." She went on to explain that Jesus had a claim on her life and that He could give her the strength and courage to take whatever came her way if she would only place her trust in Him.

For the first time, Mitzi's eyes softened.

"Do you really mean it?"

"I wouldn't lie to you, Mitzi. The Bible says He will, and I know from personal experience that He does. I have it happen in my own life."

The girl hesitated.

"But I–I've never gone to Sunday school or church much," she protested, as though afraid that would be enough to keep her from enjoying this thing that Felicia was talking about.

"That doesn't make any difference," Felicia told her. "Everybody should go to Sunday school or church, but Jesus doesn't say that you have to do so before you can become a Christian and be a child of God."

Mitzi relaxed slightly. That did make her feel better.

"The only thing you have to do is to give your life to Him and let Him make a new person of you."

Mitzi considered that thoughtfully. What Felicia said sounded wonderful, but she wasn't sure she understood exactly what she meant. While she was considering the matter, Felicia went on. Using her New Testament, she read verses to Mitzi that said that everyone is a sinner and needs to be saved.

That was something that bothered Mitzi a great deal. From somewhere, she had gotten the idea that a person could be good enough to go to heaven. And that was what she had been trying to do. If that wouldn't do any good, then she was in trouble.

Felicia went on to explain that before the flood, God provided an ark for Noah so he and his family could be saved from the fierce waters that were going to cover the earth.

"But, for us, He provided Jesus Christ. He makes it possible for us to be saved by confessing our sin and putting our trust in Jesus to save us."

"What do you mean?" Mitzi asked curiously.

"The Bible tells us that if we confess that we are

sinners and give our lives to Jesus to make a new person of us, He will do that, and we will be saved. Do you understand that?"

The girl moistened her lips. "I–I think so." In a way she did understand. In another way, she wasn't sure that she did.

But Felicia did not assume that the child knew exactly what she was talking about. Quite the contrary. Carefully, she went over the matter again, explaining in more detail God's plan for salvation. At last, Mitzi was sure that she understood and said so. Only then did the two of them kneel on the floor of the cave for prayer.

On the way back to the Rutledge Mountain Resort, Mitzi turned suddenly to Felicia.

"Does God hear us when we talk to Him?" she asked.

"Of course, He does. He not only hears us and answers our prayers, He wants us to talk to Him about the problems we have. He wants us to ask Him for help."

Mitzi brightened. "He does?"

"He does," Felicia answered.

"And He will help?" In spite of herself, there was a question in her voice, the faintest suspicion that perhaps the help of God would somehow not be available to her.

"You can be sure of it," Felicia told her fervently.

The girl's eyes gleamed.

CHAPTER 8

A CHANGED GIRL

Before they got back to the Rutledge Mountain Resort that afternoon following the rain, Felicia urged Mitzi to tell someone about her new decision to let Christ have control of her life. Mitzi listened carefully, but she wasn't sure that she liked the idea.

"Do you mean that I've *got* to tell someone?" she echoed.

"The Bible tells us that we should. But it isn't that difficult," Felicia assured her. "It isn't nearly as hard as it is to think about it."

Mitzi hesitated, the lines deepening around her young mouth.

"Who would I tell?"

"Anyone who is easy for you to talk to. Your dad or maybe your mom."

Mitzi flinched as though she had been slapped across the face.

"Oh, I couldn't tell them!" she blurted.

"Why not?" Felicia hadn't intended to ask that question. It just slipped out.

"I just couldn't," she replied evasively. "They wouldn't understand."

They rode on for half a minute or so, allowing their horses to pick their way carefully along the trail.

"Maybe you could tell your brother or sister."

"I don't have any."

"Or a good friend," Felicia suggested.

Mitzi weighed that for a time, as though trying to decide which friend she would feel free to tell what had happened to her.

"I–I'd have to wait until I get home," she said. "I don't have any good friends here."

Felicia did not press the matter further.

They were almost at the lodge before Mitzi spoke again.

"You will pray for me, won't you, Felicia?" she asked seriously.

"Of course, I will."

Felicia told Joan about Mitzi's decision to be a Christian, but neither of them said anything to anyone else about it.

"Actually," Felicia stated, "it's up to her to tell it if she wants it told."

Although there was no indication that Mitzi had mentioned her new life in Christ to anyone else, she did seem to be happier than at any time since she and her father had come to the resort. She was still shy and waited on the fringe of the activities to be asked to join in, but once she started taking part, it seemed that her inhibitions vanished. Every now and then, her laughter shrilled with the others.

"It's wonderful to see the change that's come over her," Joan said. "She's beginning to act the way the other kids do."

"I was thinking the same thing myself." The lights in Felicia's eyes flicked on. "She was even teasing us about Ted and Phil last night."

"She wasn't teasing *me,*" Joan retorted. "She didn't even mention me. What she said was that *you* were the one who wanted to go swimming all the time when a certain lifeguard was on duty."

The stain crept up into Felicia's cheeks.

"She meant you too."

"That's not what she said."

Nevertheless, both girls were relieved to see the change that had come over Mitzi. If nothing else was accomplished during their summer at the resort, they could still feel that it had been worthwhile.

The next few days were spent in a flurry of activity.

Clark and Anita Rutledge thought it would be good to have an occasional overnight trail ride for the kids. They assigned a waitress with a life-saving certificate to temporary duty as lifeguard at the pool and sent Phil and Ted up the mountain a few miles with the boys on horseback to stay for the night.

When they returned, Felicia and Joan were to do the same with the girls.

"You can handle an overnight trail ride with the girls, can't you?" Mr. Rutledge asked.

"I'm sure we can."

"I'll send Mr. Dickerson along to take care of the horses for you and give you a hand with the tents."

Felicia and Joan both agreed that it would be good to have the grizzled old wrangler along. They thought they could take care of everything without him, but it would be comforting to know that he would be within calling distance if they needed him.

The moment the ride for the boys was announced, the girls began to pester for an overnight trail ride of their own.

"We're going to get to go on a camping trip by horseback, too, aren't we?" a raven-haired eleven-year-old asked, excitement edging her voice.

Joan pretended to believe that they wouldn't want to go.

"You girls really wouldn't care about making a trip like that, would you?" With difficulty she was able to keep her face straight.

"Wouldn't we, though!"

"Those boys think they're so smart!" The girls crowded close around Joan and Felicia. "They've been boasting that we wouldn't get to go because we're too scared."

Joan's eyes widened. "Aren't you?"

"Joan Bailey," Felicia said, laughing. "You're a traitor to the cause."

"I just wanted to be sure that you all wanted to go, that's all." Her twinkling eyes said that she had just been teasing them. "We'll show those boys who's *scared!*"

A few minutes later the girls informed the boys in the group that they, too, were going to have an overnight trail ride.

"So you don't need to think that you're so smart!" one of them exclaimed indignantly.

"Felicia and Joan wouldn't take you on an overnight camping trip by horseback," Donald protested.

"They are too! You just wait and see!"

"They'd be too scared. They wouldn't even let me keep a little old garter snake. What will they do when they get all you scaredy-cat girls out in the woods where there's rattlesnakes and grizzly bears and wolves and–"

"Ask Mr. Rutledge if you don't believe us. You'll find out who's scared."

By this time, another boy had joined Donald.

"But you won't have Ted and Phil along," he said, "so you won't get to go mountain climbing." He eyed the girls quizzically to see if he had scored. "That's what we're going to get to do. We're going mountain climbing."

"Oh, pooh! We could go mountain climbing if we want to. Felicia and Joan are good mountain climbers. They go out and climb around on mountains just for fun."

That seemed to change the situation somewhat. Doubt crowded into Donald's eyes, but he couldn't argue against the girls effectively.

"How come nobody else has seen them doing all this mountain climbing if they're so good at it?" he asked defensively.

"They just don't want to show up the boys, that's all. They're too modest."

Felicia came up just then, and Donald turned to her.

"Are you a good mountain climber?" he asked.

"Me?" Her laughter rang. "I'm the greatest!"

"See!" the girl echoed. "What did I tell you? Felicia and Joan are good mountain climbers, so you don't need to think you're so smart because Ted and Phil are going to take you mountain climbing."

At that moment, Felicia Cartright became aware that the conversation had serious overtones.

"I wouldn't exactly say that I'm the greatest mountain climber in the world," she conceded.

"But you are pretty good, aren't you?"

She hesitated. "I don't know that I would be honest in saying that I'm good, either."

Disappointment edged the girl's voice. "But you have done *some* mountain climbing, haven't you, Felicia?"

Felicia winked at her.

"How about saying that I've done very well at climbing some small hills?"

Donald smirked, and the girl stuck out the tip of her tongue at him.

Felicia was telling Joan about the incident that night as they were entering the dining hall, when John Simmons approached them.

"Oh, there you are." His smile came and went. "I wondered whether I was going to be able to find you."

They turned aside with him to some easy chairs in front of the fireplace.

"Did you have something you wanted to see us about?" Joan asked when they were seated.

"As a matter of fact, I did."

He was talking to Joan but looking directly at Felicia.

She squirmed uncomfortably. He had been so bitter about God and so sure that He didn't love people if there was a God! She wondered if he had learned of Mitzi's decision and was going to express his anger about it.

Steeling herself, she waited.

But he had nothing like that in mind. Instead, he had a favor to ask of them.

"I just got word that I've got to return to Pierre early in the morning and be gone for two or three days," he began. "I talked with Clark about it, and he said that he and Anita would be glad to take care of Mitzi for me, but she doesn't want to stay with them."

"I see."

"She says that she would rather stay with you girls if she can't go along with me." He paused. "I know that's quite an imposition on you, and I certainly will understand if you decide that you would rather not."

"Oh, we wouldn't mind," Joan said quickly. "In fact, we'd love to have her. Wouldn't we, Felicia?"

"Of course."

Mr. Simmons reached for his wallet.

"That is a relief. I'll expect to pay you, of course."

"That won't be necessary," they told him.

CHAPTER 9

A CHANGE IN PLANS

Simmons was planning to leave the mountain resort for South Dakota's capital city early the next morning, so Felicia and Joan got Mitzi and took her with them to breakfast. When she came out of the room she and her father shared, her eyes were swollen suspiciously, and the veins in them showed red. For an instant, Felicia thought she had been crying, but a smile winked at the corners of her mouth, and she took her hand.

"Dad wanted me to stay with Mr. and Mrs. Rutledge," she said, "but I didn't want to do that. I wanted to stay with you."

"We want you to stay with us too," Felicia told her.

Mitzi squeezed her hand affectionately.

"Am I going to get to stay right in your room?" she asked.

"That's right. Mr. Rutledge will see that there's a rollaway bed put in for you. Won't that be nice?"

"I'm excited about it already."

At the breakfast table, Joan mentioned the trail ride they would be starting the next day.

"I'm so glad you'll be here for that," she said.

Mitzi shrugged her indifference. "I guess it will be all right."

Both Felicia and Joan eyed her critically. They had supposed she would have been excited about the overnight trail ride, but she wasn't. Actually, she acted as though she didn't care whether she went at all.

By midafternoon, the plans for the overnight ride were complete. The cooks were getting the food packed for them to take, and Joan instructed the girls to bring their sleeping bags down to the horse barn right after breakfast.

"Mr. Dickerson will be there to get the gear on the packhorses," she said, "so we can get started just as early as possible."

Young eyes sparkled with excitement. All except Mitzi, that was. She didn't seem to care whether she got to go or not.

"I can't understand her," Felicia said. "One minute I think she is more settled and happier. The next, she acts as though she's carrying all the problems in the world."

"She'll change her mind about the camping trip when we get out on the trail, I'm sure."

That evening, Mitzi was going into the dining hall with Felicia and Joan when she stopped suddenly. Her eyes widened, and she squealed with delight.

"Mom!" She tore away from the girls and went running into the arms of a woman who looked very much like her. "Oh, Mom!"

For an instant or two, they clung to each other.

"I've been so lonesome for you!"

"I've been lonesome for you, too, honey," the woman said.

By this time, they were both crying a little.

Felicia and Joan watched uneasily. They felt as though they were invading the privacy of Mitzi and her mother by standing there watching them, yet they were in charge of the girl. There was nothing else they could do.

After a time, Mrs. Simmons disengaged herself from her daughter's arms and straightened slowly, wiping away the tears. Only then did she become aware of Joan and Felicia.

"I'm Darlene Simmons," she said. There was warmth in her smile as she extended her hand.

"I suppose you are the girls Mitzi has been talking so much about."

"They're the ones." Mitzi spoke breathlessly, as though concerned that they like her mother. She introduced them both.

"Your husband had to go back to town for two

or three days," Felicia explained, "so he asked us to take care of Mitzi while he was gone."

"That's what Mrs. Rutledge told me." She put her arm around her daughter and pulled her close. "And I want to thank you both for taking care of her. She thinks a great deal of you. But I know you won't mind if I take over the responsibility now."

"Of course not," Felicia said. "We know Mitzi would much rather be with you than she would with us."

Mrs. Simmons was smiling. "We will see you girls in the morning before we leave."

Mitzi stared at her. "You mean we're going to leave tomorrow?" she asked. "We're not even going to wait until Daddy gets back?"

A cloud passed briefly over Mrs. Simmons' face. For an instant or two, it was difficult for her to speak.

"We must go," she said. "I really shouldn't have taken off the time to come now, but I felt that I had to come and get you."

The cloud that had been her mother's now dulled Mitzi's eyes. She glanced helplessly at the girls and went into the dining room with her mother.

"That is strange, isn't it?" Felicia said softly.

Joan nodded.

"It's quite a development. I was beginning to wonder if Mitzi even had a mother."

They went into the dining room and took a small table apart from the other guests.

"I guess I've been wondering about that all the

time," Felicia said, picking up her fork and holding it thoughtfully between her thumb and forefinger. "When you think about it, it's strange for a father to bring a girl Mitzi's age out to a resort like this alone when he has a wife."

"There's something strange about it," Joan answered, "but now we might never know what it's all about. She's leaving in the morning, and that will be the end of that. We won't be able to find out what's bothering her."

Felicia glanced at the table across the dining room where Mitzi and her mother were sitting.

"At least she's a Christian now. She has the Lord to help her."

The waitress came with the coffee and filled their cups. They waited until she had finished and they were alone once more.

"But," Felicia continued, "I'm still concerned about her. She has the saddest eyes I've ever seen on a girl her age."

"You can say that again. They're haunting."

The girls were still talking about Mitzi and her mother when Phil and Ted came over to them.

"It's a fine thing the way you girls hide yourselves off in a corner," Ted told them. "What is this 'table for two' business? Are you tired of our company already?"

"As a matter of fact," Felicia said, her smile flickering merrily, "we're glad to have you come along. The conversation was getting dreary."

At the invitation, the boys pulled out the chairs on the opposite sides of the table and sat down.

"What's all this dreary conversation business, anyway?" Ted asked. "Didn't you know you could talk about Phil and me?"

"And that wouldn't be dreary?" Joan asked, laughing with her eyes.

Phil groaned. "You sure know how to hurt a guy."

"For your information," Felicia said, "we weren't talking about you at all."

"You weren't?" Ted echoed. "That's even worse."

"We were talking over something very confidentially. That's why we chose this cozy little corner."

"Something confidential?" Ted still seemed to think it was a joke. "Like what?"

"If we told you what we were talking about," Joan put in, "it wouldn't be confidential anymore, now would it?"

"But you don't know how good I am at keeping confidential secrets. If you'll give me a few minutes, I'll tell you all the secrets I know."

"That's what I call most thoughtful," Felicia said, bringing her laughter under control so she could speak.

By this time, Mitzi and her mother had finished eating and got to their feet to leave. The boys saw her wave shyly at Felicia and Joan.

"We thought you were going to be taking care of the Simmons girl for a couple of days," Phil said.

"So did we," Joan answered, "but there was a

change in plans. Her mother came out unexpectedly, so she's with her."

"And now," Felicia added, "she's going to take her home the first thing in the morning, so she'll miss out on the overnight trail ride."

For a brief space of time, the boys were silent.

"I can't help feeling sorry for that little girl," Ted said finally. "Have you noticed her at the swimming pool, Phil?"

"I watched her a while yesterday afternoon. She didn't seem to be enjoying herself much."

"She doesn't join in with the other kids at all."

Felicia and Joan said nothing, but they were surprised to hear the boys talking the way they were. They hadn't realized that Mitzi's unhappiness was so obvious.

"I can hardly bear the thought of having her leave when she's so upset," Felicia observed when she and Joan were in their room putting up their hair before going to bed. "I keep thinking we ought to be doing something to help her."

"I feel the same way myself. But there's nothing we can do about it. Her mother's here and is going to take her away in the morning." Joan looked at herself in the mirror critically. "So, that's that."

There was a long, painful silence.

"We'll have to be sure to pray for her every day," Felicia said.

CHAPTER 10

AN OVERNIGHT TRAIL RIDE

C oncern and frustration still disturbed Felicia and
Joan as they went in to breakfast the following
morning. They were still thinking about Mitzi and
the haunting look in her somber young face that was
far older than her years. They were just finding a
table when Mrs. Simmons came over to them briskly.

"Good morning."

They returned her greeting.

"Are you and Mitzi leaving now?" Felicia asked.
She looked around, realizing that she hadn't told
the girl goodbye.

"That's what I wanted to talk with you about before
Mitzi comes in. May I sit down?"

"Of course," Joan told her.

When they were seated, Mrs. Simmons continued. "We were planning to go this morning right
after breakfast, but Mitzi is so anxious to go on this

overnight trail ride that she has practically persuaded me to wait until she makes the trip."

"That would be nice," Felicia said.

"Then it would be all right for her to go?"

"We'd *love* to have her."

Mrs. Simmons was obviously relieved.

"That's splendid. She was so upset last night at the thought of missing the camping trip that I decided to wait until you get back tomorrow afternoon. Another day isn't going to make too much difference in my plans."

Mitzi came into the dining room after a minute or two and approached their table, questions glittering in her eyes. "Is it all right, Mom?" she asked. "Is it okay if I go on the trail ride with Felicia and Joan and the girls?"

Mrs. Simmons smiled indulgently. "Everything is arranged, my dear."

"Oh, good! I was afraid I wouldn't be able to go after we said we were going to leave this morning."

She would have left the dining room then, but her mother stopped her.

"You haven't eaten yet, Mitzi. You should have something to eat before you go."

"I can't, Mom. I don't have time. I've got to get my bedroll and some clothes and everything. I don't have a minute's time to waste if I'm going to be ready by the time the others are."

"I don't think we'll be going quite that soon," Felicia

told her. "You'll be able to get packed, so you won't delay us, even if you take the time to eat breakfast."

"But I'm really not all that hungry," she protested. Nevertheless, she sat down and ordered breakfast. As soon as she finished eating, she pushed back from the table.

"I've got to run. Be seeing you." With that, she scurried away.

It was not until Mitzi was out of hearing that Mrs. Simmons spoke again. "It's very nice of you to allow Mitzi to make the trip today."

"We're only glad that she could come."

For the space of half a minute or so, silence engulfed them.

"I'm so happy that she has found something she enjoys," Mrs. Simmons said at last. "I'm afraid Mitzi has had a difficult time of it lately."

"We've noticed that she's seemed unhappy." Joan let the sentence hang there, waiting for Mrs. Simmons to explain why her daughter was so sad.

But the older woman did not continue. Instead, she stood and held out her hand. "I want to thank you girls so very much for the interest you've taken in Mitzi. I'll always be grateful for it."

Strangely enough, Mitzi's excitement over the camping trip they were starting that morning seemed to vanish as soon as she was out of her mother's sight. Her smile gave way to deep frown lines that made her look as though she was about to cry, and the lights in her eyes dulled. She mounted her horse and rode indifferently, as though she didn't care whether she kept up with the others or not. Two or three times, Martin Dickerson had to stop the others to wait for Mitzi to catch up.

"You're going to have to ride a little faster," he said mildly, "or we're not going to get there in time to pitch camp before dark."

Felicia went back and rode beside her. Mitzi glanced in her direction but did not speak.

"Is there something troubling you?" Felicia asked after a time, gently.

Mitzi's scowl told Felicia that she wished to be left alone.

"I'm all right," she said.

Felicia knew the girl didn't want to continue the conversation, but she couldn't stop now. Mitzi's bewilderment and sadness were so evident.

"I'd like to help you."

The girl's voice raised testily. "I'm all right, I tell you! Just leave me alone!"

Felicia's gaze met hers and held there. She could have allowed herself to be hurt by the outburst but not if she wanted to help Mitzi. In an instant or two, the girl's expression changed.

"I'm sorry, Felicia," she said, near tears. "But I'm all right. Honestly, I am."

Felicia's smile invited trust and confidence. "Whenever you want to talk to me, Mitzi, just remember that I'll always be glad to help in any way I can."

Mitzi's eyes were luminous, but she did not reply.

They picked their way slowly around the mountain past a sheer granite cliff that thrust itself upward at least two hundred feet and forded two narrow mountain streams. Now and then, as they passed a narrow opening in the trees, they could see the village of Silver City lying far below them in the valley.

In one such spot, Mitzi, who was bringing up the rear and usually lagged some distance behind the others, reined in. When Felicia stopped and turned in the saddle to see her, the girl was sitting motionless, her hands wrapped around the saddle horn as she stared down at the quiet mountain town.

Felicia longed to go back and put her arms around the girl, but she knew it would be useless for her to try to do so. At least at the moment.

They stopped for sandwiches at noon, and by three o'clock, they had reached their campsite. The girls pitched their small tents and built a campfire while the wrangler unsaddled their horses and fed them.

It was an exciting experience for the girls, and they were enjoying even the routine duties of making camp, pitching tents, and carrying wood and water.

During the campfire service after supper, Felicia missed Mitzi. She got up and went to look for her.

At first, she thought the girl had probably gone back to her tent in an effort to be alone. But when she wasn't there, Felicia went down by the mountain stream. She didn't know why she thought to look there, except that it seemed to her she would probably go to a place like that if she were Mitzi's age and wanted to be alone.

In a few minutes, she found the girl sitting on a big rock, her knees pulled up under her chin and her head down.

Felicia spoke to her.

She answered her greeting without looking up.

For a moment or two, Felicia remained silent. Then she sat down quietly beside the girl.

"What is it, Mitzi?" she asked, her voice almost a whisper. "What's troubling you?"

The girl acted as though she hadn't even heard her.

Felicia put her arm around her. Mitzi did not respond. Neither did she pull away.

"Don't try to battle your problems alone. Why don't we talk to God about them?"

Mitzi raised her head, defiance glinting beneath her tears – defiance and bewilderment.

"I have been talking to God about them," she exclaimed, "but it hasn't done any good!" Bitterness was creeping in.

"Don't say that," Felicia told her.

"But it's true!" Mitzi was crying now, thin, agonizing sobs that shook her shoulders convulsively. "I don't know why God won't let me have *both* my mom and my dad!"

So that was it! Felicia should have known it was something like that. Mr. Simmons had come up to the resort with Mitzi alone. Then he had to leave for a couple of days, and his wife showed up. They were probably divorced or close to it. That explained why Mitzi was so troubled. Felicia could understand it all then.

She waited until Mitzi's sobbing began to slack off before she spoke. When she did, a tense, expectant hush muted her voice.

"God doesn't promise to answer our prayers just the way we want them answered or when we think they ought to be answered," she said, keeping her voice low. "But He does answer our prayers. I know that from personal experience. Let's tell Him how you feel about this divorce and how anxious you are that you have your parents back together and both of them at home again."

"Do you think it will do any good?" Doubt crept into her voice.

"Of course, it will."

They knelt on the bank of the mountain stream and began to pray quietly. When they had finished, Mitzi wiped her eyes.

"Do you feel any better now?"

"I think so." She raised her head to look deep into Felicia's blue eyes. "You won't tell anyone about this, will you?" she asked. "I'd just die if any of the kids found it out."

"I won't tell anyone if you don't want me to," Felicia assured her. "Is it all right if I tell Joan?"

Mitzi shook her head. "I don't want anyone else to know. Not even Joan."

Felicia didn't like the idea of keeping something from her best friend. They had never had any secrets from each other since they first began to run around together when Joan enrolled at Wellington.

But she couldn't violate Mitzi's trust either. She had given the girl her word that she wouldn't say anything about the fact that her parents were separated or divorced. As much as she would have liked to tell Joan, she determined to keep it to herself.

As soon as the campfire service was over, Joan and Felicia insisted that their young charges go to bed. They knew that the girls would be up at dawn and that they had to have their rest.

"Where did you find Mitzi?" Joan asked as soon as she and Felicia were alone together.

"Down by the stream." She spoke guardedly, knowing that she would have to be careful, or she would betray Mitzi's trust without realizing it.

"Did she say why she ran off the way she did?"

"She was feeling bad," Felicia said, "but we had a long talk, and I prayed with her. She seemed to feel better after that."

Joan noticed her evasiveness.

"Now wait a minute. Just exactly what are you trying to keep from me, anyway?" she demanded.

Felicia looked up. "Am I trying to keep something from you?"

"You just know you are."

"If I'm trying to keep something from you," Felicia told her, "did it ever occur to you that it must be a secret?"

Joan exploded indignantly.

"A secret! You can't do this to me!"

"I wish I could tell you, Joan," Felicia continued, "but I can't. Mitzi made me promise that I wouldn't tell anyone what she told me."

"But I'm your best friend."

"As soon as I can let you know, I will. Believe me."

"Just you wait until I find out something you want to know, Felicia Cartright. I'll remember this night! I promise!"

"If you were in my place, you'd do the same as I'm doing."

Joan smiled. "I suppose I would, but I can't say that I like being on *this* end of a secret."

Felicia and Joan waited until the girls were in their tents and quiet before going to bed themselves.

"Do you think Mitzi is going to be able to solve her problems, Felicia?" Joan asked after a time.

"I don't know." There was a long, painful silence. "I just don't know. But please pray for her. She needs help."

Felicia was praying silently that God would restore the Simmons home so Mitzi could have her mother and father together again when she drifted off to sleep. She didn't know whether she had been sleeping an hour or three times that long when she was awakened by a frantic cry outside their pup tent.

"Miss Cartright! Miss Bailey! Come quick!"

Instantly, the girls were awake.

"What is it?" They scrambled out of their sleeping bags. "What's the matter?"

"It's Mitzi! I looked over at her sleeping bag just now, and she wasn't there! She's gone!"

CHAPTER 11

THE MISSING GIRL

Felicia and Joan stared incredulously at the girl who had been in the same tent with Mitzi. This wasn't true. It couldn't be. It was some horrible joke or nightmare that would be over in a moment, leaving them shaken by the experience.

"Are you sure?" Joan demanded, as though her doubt could make it false.

"You can come and look for yourself." The girl's voice bordered on hysteria.

By this time the others in the party were awake and frightened.

"What is it?" Heads popped curiously out of pup tents. "What's happened?" "What's wrong?"

"There's nothing to be alarmed about," Joan said, trying to evidence a confidence she did not feel. "Mitzi probably couldn't sleep and went out for a little walk. I'm sure there is nothing to be alarmed about."

"Mitzi!" one of the girls cried. "Do you mean that Mitzi's gone?"

"She's gone all right," her tentmate repeated. "I woke up and turned over, and she wasn't there!"

Felicia and Joan looked at each other with growing helplessness. They were as disturbed as any of the girls, possibly more so because they knew that Mitzi was having problems of one sort or another. But they could not let the girls know how concerned they were.

"It's very late," Felicia told them. "You had all better go back into your tents and go to sleep. Everything is going to be all right."

"Go back to sleep?" one girl echoed. "We can't go back to sleep now, after what's happened! I'm afraid even to shut my eyes."

"So am I."

They were all up, huddled in front of the tents, shivering in their pajamas.

Felicia surveyed the situation quickly. The girls would go back to bed if she or Joan insisted on it, but that didn't mean they would go to sleep. They would just lie there talking and letting their imaginations run wild. It was better for them to be doing something – anything – rather than thinking about Mitzi and wondering what had happened to her.

"Okay," she said, "why don't you all get dressed and gather some more wood and build a fire?"

"Do you mean it?"

"But I'm sure that by the time the fire is built, we will have found Mitzi," she said, hoping she sounded calm and unconcerned.

Joan came over to her.

"What do you think we ought to do now?" She spoke in a whisper.

"It's one thirty." The corners of her mouth tightened. "I think we'd better waken Mr. Dickerson and see if he'll go and look for her."

Joan nodded. "In short, you don't buy that bit about Mitzi going for a walk because she couldn't sleep, do you?"

Felicia shook her head. "At first, I thought it might be true, but the more I think about it, the more sure I am that it can't be true. She must have gone off somewhere."

"Think she could have taken one of the horses?" Joan asked.

"Mr. Dickerson will know about that."

The girls went into their tent and dressed quickly. While Felicia got the girls using their flashlights to gather wood, Joan went down by the stream where the wrangler had tethered the horses and spread out his own bedroll. He had been awakened by the noise in camp and met her about halfway.

"What's the trouble?" he wanted to know quickly.

"It's one of the girls," Joan said. "Her tentmate found her gone."

He whistled his surprise. "It's that dreamy-eyed one, isn't it? The one we had to keep waiting on today?"

Joan nodded. "We thought perhaps she had just wandered down by the stream because she couldn't sleep; but if she had, she ought to have been back by this time."

"That little gal has been a time bomb waiting to explode," he said. "My guess is that she got mad about something and decided to run away."

He was finishing the job of buttoning his jacket as he talked to her.

"I'll go back and get my flashlight and look around," he said. "The chances are that she hasn't gone far."

"That's what Felicia and I thought."

"You and that partner of yours had better stay with the girls and keep them quiet and out of trouble. If they get so shaken up they try to go out and find her themselves, we might wind up with the whole bunch of them lost."

Joan did as she was told.

As soon as she got back, the girls saw her and crowded around, plying her with questions.

"Did you find her?" "Where did you go?" "What are we going to do?" Questions came from everyone in the group.

"If you'll all be quiet so I can make you hear, I'll tell you everything I know."

They quieted, tensely.

"Mr. Dickerson has gone out looking for Mitzi, but he wants to be sure that we all stay in camp so no one else gets lost and complicates matters."

"Does he have any idea what happened to her? Does he know where she is?"

"The chances are that she isn't far away," Joan told them. "And that, actually, is all I know."

"And what will happen if he doesn't find her?" one of the girls broke in, near hysteria.

"If he doesn't find her, he'll probably ride back to the resort to get Mr. Rutledge and the forest ranger and some of the men to help look for her. He did say that he doesn't believe she is very far away."

Several of the girls started to cry.

"Now, listen," Felicia ordered sternly. "Tears aren't going to help Mitzi now. The only way we can help her is to keep good control of ourselves."

Someone made a strange noise as she tried to stifle a sob.

"Let's get the fire built up so it isn't so cold."

Having something to do seemed to help the girls get their minds on something other than Mitzi. They built up the fire and began to pile wood beside it until finally even Felicia and Joan had to admit that it was useless for them to gather more fuel for a time. Once the work was done, they huddled miserably around the yellow flames.

"Why did she run away?" someone asked. "I thought–"

Before anyone could answer, the wrangler rode into camp. A hush fell expectantly over the group.

"I've looked around here for Mitzi," he told Felicia

and Joan quietly. "But I haven't been able to find her. I think I'd better go in to get Mr. Rutledge and some other help. I want all of you to stay here until I get back."

He lifted the reins, and his mount started forward.

No one spoke until the horse's hoofbeats died away.

"Something terrible is going to happen to Mitzi," one girl clamored tearfully. "I just know it!"

Felicia got to her feet.

"I think the best thing we can do right now," she said, "is to talk with God about this. We've been telling you each day how important it is that we pray regularly for the things we need. Now, something has come up that gives us a chance to put into practice some of the things that we have been talking about."

She went back to her own pup tent, got her Bible, and, in the glow of the fire, opened it to the book of John and began to read. She read them a number of verses about prayer and how Jesus urged His followers to pray for their needs.

"Now, let's bow our heads and ask God to keep Mitzi safe from harm and to help us to find her real soon."

After the girls had spent some time in prayer, they seemed to feel better, yet they sat around the fire talking in low tones or staring silently at the flames. Felicia and Joan felt the same as the girls they were taking care of. In fact, they felt as bad as though they had been the cause of what had happened to Mitzi.

The silence hung about them as impenetrable as the night, except that, every now and then, one of the girls would think she heard the men from the resort coming to look for Mitzi. Felicia and Joan, however, knew that they could not be back so soon. Mr. Dickerson would ride much faster alone, but even then, the search party could not be expected for another hour or so. All they could do was wait.

After a time, one of the girls began to sob quietly.

"Susan," Joan exclaimed firmly. "What is the matter?"

The girl looked up. "It's Mitzi!" she blurted. "I'm afraid that something terrible has happened to her!"

"Stop that crying. The search party will be here before long, and they will go out and find her. Crying will only make things worse."

Susan sat erect, struggling to keep back the tears. Felicia knew exactly how Susan felt. She had difficulty herself in not crying.

The inactivity was the worst. If only they could be doing something!

She knew how frightened Mitzi must be out on the mountain alone at night. The poor girl must be terrified.

Felicia got to her feet and stood for a moment or two, her gaze fixed on the curtain of blackness that surrounded them. A thin cloud layer hid the stars, making the night even darker than usual.

For the moment, she fought against the almost uncontrollable impulse to go running off into the night to look for Mitzi on her own. Only the knowledge that she and Joan had the rest of the girls to look after restrained her.

The night was wasting, and the first softening of the blackness was evident when they heard the unmistakable sounds of vehicles approaching.

"They're coming!" Susan cried, scrambling to her feet. "They're coming!"

A moment later a jeep jounced noisily up to their camp, the headlights stabbing through the dark to bathe their tents in their garish yellow beams. The girls surged forward noisily, all trying to talk at once as Clark Rutledge, the forest ranger for the area, and Mrs. Simmons arrived.

Felicia and Joan tried desperately to quiet them, but it was no use, at least for the moment. Mrs. Simmons approached Felicia tearfully.

"I should never have let her come," she sobbed. "I should never have let her come!"

The forest ranger brought quiet to the excited little group.

"Quiet!" His commanding voice rang out above the others, and gradually, they fell silent. "We've got to get this search organized as quickly as possible so we can find the girl before she gets herself into real trouble."

Mrs. Simmons started to sniffle again.

"I want one of you to tell me exactly what happened," he continued, ignoring Mrs. Simmons' crying. "And don't leave out a thing."

Joan explained how unhappy and preoccupied Mitzi seemed all day, how she had gone off by herself during the campfire service, and how Felicia had gone and found her and brought her back.

"And when I woke up in the night, she was gone!" Susan blurted.

"Is that the way it was?"

Joan nodded.

"Mitzi came back with Felicia and seemed to be all right, except that she was a little quieter than usual. But Sue missed her during the night and came to tell us."

Before they had finished talking, two more jeep-loads of men and women arrived to help. Phil and Ted were among them, their mountain climbing ropes and gear in the back of one of the vehicles.

The two boys went directly to Felicia and Joan.

"What happened?" Phil asked. "When did you miss her?"

Before either of them could answer him, the ranger spoke again.

"Everybody's here, so we'd just as well move out!" he said crisply. "I want you men to go by twos. Follow your maps carefully and mark the places you've been. This search has to cover the whole area carefully, or we may miss her."

He checked to be sure that each pair of men had a revolver or rifle along to fire for signaling and sent them out.

"What do you want us to do?" one of the women asked.

He paused.

"Look after these girls, for one thing," he told her, "and see that we have something hot to eat and plenty of coffee when we come in."

Mrs. Simmons was starting to cry again. Anita Rutledge went over and put her arm around her tenderly.

"Come over here and sit down."

She allowed herself to be led to a spot near the fire and sat down on a log. "My husband," she said. "Has anybody notified my husband?"

"Someone at the resort will get in touch with him."

A sob choked in Mrs. Simmons' throat. Felicia turned quickly away, unable to look at the girl's distraught mother.

Somehow, she felt that it was their fault, that Mitzi would still be in camp if she and Joan had done a better job of watching over her or of talking to her. Felicia felt the muscles in her throat constrict. Why didn't she see that Mitzi was so upset that something terrible was going to happen? Why didn't she and Joan take the girl into their tent with them for the night? Why did they let her come along in the first place? Questions, unanswered, churned through her mind.

But all the self-accusation wouldn't change anything. Mitzi was gone! And now they didn't know whether she would ever be found again!

CHAPTER 12

THE SEARCH

Mrs. Rutledge managed to get Mrs. Simmons quieted, and the women who had come along started breakfast. By the time dawn weakened the light of the fire, everyone had eaten, and the dishes were done. Felicia left the tense little group and walked down to the stream where she stood in silence, staring into the swirling, turbulent water.

Never had she felt so helpless, so miserable.

There should have been some way for her and Joan to have anticipated trouble with Mitzi and avoided it. They had been placed in charge of the kids at the resort but had failed to take care of them the way they should have. She and Joan were responsible for what had happened. Mr. Rutledge and the others were just too kind to say anything about it. But that didn't ease the pain.

Closing her eyes, she tried to pray, but for some

reason, she could not. It was as though her prayers could go no higher than the trees around her.

Felicia still had not moved when Joan came down to join her.

"I looked all over for you," she said quietly. "I was beginning to think that you had run away too."

Felicia raised her fear-glazed eyes to study Joan's somber face.

"You know that we're responsible for this, don't you?" she asked.

Joan frowned. "I don't think so. We didn't make Mitzi run away. In fact, you did everything you could to help her."

"That's not true. We ought to have seen how upset she was and made her stay in our tent last night."

Joan touched Felicia on the arm. "Don't blame yourself this way. Nobody else does."

She did not answer her.

After a moment or two, the girls sat down on the bank of the stream, aimlessly tossing pebbles into the churning water.

"You know," Felicia said at last, "it seems to me that there's something we forgot to tell the ranger. Something that's very important."

"Like what?"

Felicia picked up a small stone and held it thoughtfully. "I don't know for sure. I've been trying to go over everything in my own mind, to see if we did tell him everything we should have told him."

Joan thought about that. "Maybe we did forget something," she said, "but I can't remember it."

Felicia would not let the matter rest so easily however.

"Mitzi was the last girl in line on the trail," she said, "and we had to stop several times to wait for her to catch up with us."

"That's right, but I don't see—"

"And when I went back to see what was taking her so long, she was sitting on her horse staring down at Silver City so intently she didn't even know I was anywhere around."

"She was probably staring off into space and not even seeing the village."

Felicia shook her head.

"I'm convinced that she was looking down at the little town."

"But why?" Joan was insistent. "Mitzi wouldn't have any reason to be interested in that village. There's hardly anything there except the general store and a filling station and the post office."

"I know all of that." The conviction came on Felicia slowly. She tossed the stone away and got to her feet. "But she was interested in it just the same. And that's one direction the ranger didn't send a search party."

Joan's eyes narrowed.

"And what do you figure on doing about that?"

"We're going out and look for her!" Felicia hadn't realized until that moment what she was thinking of. "We're going to find the trail that goes down the mountain to Silver City and follow it!"

Joan gasped. "You can't be serious! It's fifteen miles to that village!"

"It's no farther for us than it is for Mitzi." Felicia turned on her heel. "And the quicker we get going, the shorter the distance we'll have to walk."

"You know that forest ranger isn't going to like it if we go traipsing off into the woods on our own. He told us to stay in camp."

"He was talking about the *little* girls," Felicia countered. "He said they should stay in camp so they don't get lost."

"You just wait and see who he was talking about."

"I'm not going to worry about it." Felicia tossed her head defiantly. "There's nothing he can *do* about it after we're gone."

Resignation deepened the frown lines about her face. "If you're determined to go, I guess I don't have any choice," she said. "I'll have to go along and keep you out of trouble."

Back in camp, Felicia told Mrs. Rutledge about Mitzi's preoccupation with Silver City and her guess that the girl may have tried to get there for some reason.

"It scarcely seems likely that a girl of her age would try to get to a little place like that," the woman said, "but I suppose it is possible."

"Then you think it would be all right for us to go?"

Mrs. Rutledge's lips pursed momentarily.

"I don't see why not," she said at last. "Only I'd suggest that you take your horses. You'll be able to go so much faster."

They saddled their mounts hurriedly and rode out of camp.

"At least we're on horseback," Joan said. "And that's an improvement over going all the way down the mountain on foot."

"And," Felicia added, "Mrs. Rutledge said it was all right for us to go, so that takes care of the forest ranger."

"It probably means that *she'll* get shot instead of you and me."

"I'd run that risk if I thought it would help us to find Mitzi and get her back safely."

Both Felicia and Joan found that they felt better doing something rather than sitting around. They rode down the narrow, twisting trail carefully, looking for some sign that Mitzi had used the trail in leaving the camp.

"The ground's too hard to hold any footprints," Felicia said. In spite of herself, her own uneasiness and doubt began to take root and sprout. "And the path's too wide for her to break branches accidentally as she walked."

"And maybe she didn't go along this path. Did you ever think of that?"

Felicia did not reply. She knew that was a possibility. In fact, now it seemed foolish even to go down a trail on such flimsy evidence as they had. But they couldn't just stand around waiting. They had to be doing something to help.

They rode on in comparative silence.

After a time, the trail began to narrow perceptibly. Both girls noticed it, but it was several minutes later before either mentioned what was happening. At last Felicia, who was in the lead, reined her horse to a halt. The brush on either side of the trail was touching her legs.

"I don't like this, Joan," she said, an ominous tone creeping into her voice. "I don't like it at all."

"Do you suppose it gets wider after we get a bit farther down the mountain?"

"I don't know." She spoke slowly. "It doesn't look to me as though this trail is being used at all."

Joan's mouth crinkled. "Do you suppose that we missed a turn somewhere?"

Felicia shook her head. "I didn't see it if we did."

For the space of half a minute or so, they sat motionless on their horses, staring at the dwindling, brush-choked trail ahead.

"I think we'd just as well turn around and go back, don't you?"

Joan nodded. "There doesn't seem to be any reason for going–" Her voice choked. "Felicia!" she cried, pointing. "Look at this! Did you break this twig?"

"I don't think so."

She swung quickly off her horse and examined it. The edges of the break had already started to dry, so it couldn't have been done within the last two or three minutes. That meant they hadn't broken it. But neither had it turned brown, so it hadn't been done a long while before.

"Do you suppose Mitzi could have broken it as she came this way?"

Felicia nodded. What other reason could there be for the broken twig?

Excitement mounting, she got on her saddle horse once more and urged him forward, with Joan close behind. The horses didn't like the way the brush crowded in against them, and once or twice, Felicia's mount stopped stubbornly and wanted to turn. She kicked him with her heels, forcing him forward.

Another hundred yards and Felicia saw a second broken branch. This one Mitzi *must* have stepped on. Felicia wanted to kick her horse to a gallop, but that was impossible. The trail ribboned through the thick brush, dwindling as it went, until the horses could not go farther. Even their determined riders realized as much. The tangle of brush and trees was almost too formidable for a person to go through.

"Now what do we do?" Joan asked.

Before Felicia could answer, a faint cry drifted to them.

"What was that?'

The only sound was that of the wind kissing the leaves.

"I thought I heard someone," Joan whispered.

The silence was deafening.

"So did I," Felicia said, trying to quiet the excited pounding of her heart.

CHAPTER 13

A DANGEROUS SPOT!

Felicia and Joan leaned forward intently, trying the silence with their ears. Although they waited for the second cry, they were unprepared for it when it came, sounding in faintly from somewhere ahead.

It was weak and so blurred by distance that they could have been excused for not recognizing it as human at all. Indeed, they might have missed it completely had it not been that they were prepared for it by the broken branches and the cry of a few moments before.

"It's Mitzi!" Felicia whispered, her voice tense with emotion.

Swinging off her startled saddle horse, she wrapped the reins around a sapling nearby and tied them deftly. Joan did the same. Then the girls rushed forward.

"Mitzi!" Felicia cried as she stumbled through the brush. "Mitzi!"

There was no answer, but they couldn't have heard it if there had been, they were crashing so noisily through the forest. Felicia caught her toe on a root and sprawled forward, skinning her knee and bruising her cheek. But she scrambled to her feet and hurried on.

Half a minute later, they were out of the forest, stopped by a formidable granite wall that plunged downward halfway to the base of the mountain and stretched upward as though to embrace the sky.

"Oh!" The cry involuntarily escaped Felicia's lips. There was Mitzi one hundred feet or so out on the cliff, clinging to the sheer rock face precariously.

"Dear God!" Felicia cried inwardly, terror freezing her body. "Help Mitzi not to be scared and–and help us to get her back safely."

"Mitzi!" She spoke just loudly enough so the girl could hear. "Mitzi!"

"Felicia!" Hope mingled with the panic in her voice. "I prayed and prayed that you would come!"

Joan grasped Felicia's hand with icy fingers and squeezed it until it ached.

"Now, Mitzi," Felicia began, not knowing how she was able to keep her voice so calm. "Be very careful and do exactly as I tell you to."

"All right. I didn't mean to get into a place like this. I was just going down to Silver City when I came to this–this place, and it was so dark I couldn't see where I was or anything, so I was going to go across it the way Ted and Phil do. But–" Her voice trailed off to nothing.

"Don't talk about that now. I want you to try to move this way, Mitzi – very carefully. Move your left foot first."

The terrified girl tried to do as she was told, but she could not. Fear gripped her and held her paralyzed.

"I can't do it, Felicia! I'll fall!"

Felicia spoke sharply. "You aren't going to fall, Mitzi. Don't talk that way."

Joan touched her arm. "Don't say anything to Mitzi," she said softly, "but I'm going back to the camp for help. She's not going to be able to get off of that ledge alone."

Felicia nodded. "But hurry! She's so frightened she might not be able to stay there very long."

Almost silently, Joan disappeared into the forest.

"Felicia!" The terror crept back into her voice. "Felicia! You aren't leaving, are you?"

"No, I'm right here!"

"Who was that talking to you just now?"

"It was only Joan. She rode along with me to find you!"

The silence was deafening.

"Felicia!" Mitzi's voice grew taut and broke.

"I'm right here!" Then she realized that she was going to have to keep the girl's mind off the place where she was. "Why did you leave camp, Mitzi?" she asked. "We've been looking everywhere for you."

"I was just going down to Silver City to call my daddy and–and talk to him."

"He was going to be back at the resort tonight," Felicia reminded her.

"But I wouldn't be there. Mom was going to take me away before he got back, and he's going to South America to a new job right away, and I–I might never get to see him again!"

"I see."

Mitzi's fingers started to slip.

"Felicia!" Her cry was shrill and piercing. "I can't hang on any longer! I'm going to fall!"

Felicia saw that the girl's fingers were slipping slightly as she tried to dig them into the granite cliff, and her toes were on a narrow ledge scarcely six inches wide. She couldn't risk waiting until Joan got back with help. Whatever was done would have to be done immediately.

"Hang on, Mitzi," she ordered crisply. "I'm coming out to help you!"

Felicia extended one foot uneasily, shuddering as she looked down at the granite rubble and brush at the base of the cliff several hundred feet below. She couldn't go out on that ledge, she reasoned. If she did, she would be in the same predicament Mitzi was. But, if she didn't, what would happen to Mitzi?

With a prayer in her heart, Felicia stepped resolutely out on the ledge. Sweat moistened the palms of her hands, and her legs trembled so violently she was afraid she wasn't going to be able to make them move.

"Hurry, Felicia!" Mitzi stammered. "I–I can't hang on any longer!" Her cry was a thin, plaintive whimper. "I can't do it! My hands are slipping! I'm going to fall!"

Felicia's voice was so harsh and stern it didn't even sound like hers. "You've got to hang on, Mitzi!" she snapped. "You can't let go now! I'm coming out to get you!"

That seemed to quiet the girl momentarily, but Felicia knew it would only last a brief time. She would have to reach her right away, or she would panic and let go.

Grimly, Felicia forced herself to slide her foot along the narrow shelf. At first, the going was comparatively easy. True, the shelf for her feet was not very wide, but it was wide enough to give her the feeling of security. And there was a rough outcropping about the height of her head, to furnish good handholds. Her first thought was that of relief. It wasn't going to be as bad as she thought it was.

Now she could see why Mitzi had tackled the cliff in the first place. She had come upon it in the semi-darkness of early morning when the mountain was wrapped in mist and the curtain of the night. She couldn't have known that the granite wall fell away for several hundred feet.

If Mitzi had only kept going, Felicia reasoned,

she would probably have reached the other side. She must have looked down and panicked.

Felicia moved forty or fifty feet easily and was beginning to think she would reach the frightened girl without difficulty.

Gradually, however, the ledge she was inching her feet along began to narrow. She felt the sharp edge through the sole of her tennis shoes half along her heel. A piece of the ledge the size of a baseball broke off under her foot and she started suddenly, tightening her grip with her hands.

For an instant, fear immobilized her. She *had* to go back, she reasoned desperately. No one could blame her for not going on.

But Mitzi's whimpered pleading for help drifted over to her. To stop would surely send the girl to her death! The choice was no longer Felicia's to make. Whatever happened, she had to go on!

Ten or fifteen feet farther, the ledge widened, and she sighed her relief. But it was only for a moment, the length of time it took her to move across a dozen feet. Then the ledge narrowed until she wondered whether there was enough of it extending beyond the wall so she dared to rest her weight on it.

Every breath was a desperate prayer for help and strength and courage. Every move was a test of faith. She pressed her lithe young body against the cliff as tightly as possible.

"Felicia!" the girl cried. "I'm falling! I'm falling!"

"No, you're not! Hang on! I'm coming as fast as I can!"

Another few feet and she was close enough to reach out with her hand and touch the terror-stricken girl.

"You did come!"

Mitzi clutched for her hand. Felicia drew it away quickly, almost losing her balance as she did so.

"Don't do that! We'll both fall!"

"I–I'm sorry!"

For the space of half a minute or so, they clung there frantically, the strength drained from their trembling legs.

Felicia knew that they could not stay there long. Every minute that passed made them less able to cope with the treacherous cliff.

"Mitzi," she said at last, "I want you to do exactly as I say."

"A-a-all right."

"I'm right here beside you, and I'm not going to let you fall, so move your left foot this way."

"I–I can't!"

"Yes, you can" Felicia was stern. "Do as I tell you! Your left foot! Pick it up and move it this way. That's it. A little farther. There." She moistened her lips with the tip of her tongue. "Now move your left hand about the same distance."

Mitzi did as Felicia ordered. Then Felicia had her move her right hand and her right foot.

"See, that wasn't so bad."

The girl was breathing heavily.

"Now, let's do it again."

Felicia managed to slide back along the cliff a foot or so.

It was almost as hard to get Mitzi to take the second step as it was to get her to take the first, but she made that one too. It seemed to give her a bit more confidence.

"That's it," Felicia told her. "Keep coming now. Don't stop. Just a few more steps."

Movement, in itself, seemed to lend strength and courage to Mitzi. That and Felicia's calm voice and quiet assurance that everything was going to be all right.

At last, Felicia was off the cliff herself. She reached out her hand, took Mitzi's, and pulled her to safety. A prayer of thankfulness swept through her as she enveloped Mitzi in her arms.

They both cried their relief.

CHAPTER 14

A NEW START

Felicia and Mitzi were still wrapped in each other's arms when Joan came rushing back with Mr. and Mrs. Simmons, the forest ranger, and Phil and Ted. Mitzi's mother was the first to reach them. She started to sob hysterically when she saw that Mitzi was off the cliff and was all right. Mr. Simmons was crying too, silently.

Mitzi disengaged herself from Felicia and put her arms around both her mother and father, sobbing until her shoulders shook.

Joan knelt beside Felicia.

"How did you do it?" she asked quietly. "I was sure she wouldn't be able to move a step."

Felicia dried her eyes. "It wasn't easy," she said. "Believe me."

Joan was staring at her hands.

"What did you do to your fingers?"

Only then did Felicia realize that they were cut and bleeding.

After a time, the forest ranger came over to Felicia. "I don't know what you did to get her to move, young lady, but we all owe you a vote of thanks. When your friend told me where she was, I didn't think anyone would have a chance of getting her off the cliff alive."

He noted the time.

"We'd better get back to the others, hadn't we?" he asked.

The horses and gear had to be taken back to the resort, but Mr. Rutledge sent the girls and Mitzi and her parents back in the jeeps. Ted and Phil were directed to take the horses and camping equipment back to the lodge. The group was about to leave when Mr. Simmons asked the driver to wait a minute.

"I want to go over and see Felicia Cartright before we leave," he said.

The driver nodded.

"Felicia." Mr. Simmons' voice was strangely taut when he approached the vehicle the girls were to ride in.

"Yes?" She turned to look at him.

"I–I–" He had difficulty in saying what was on his heart. "I don't know how I can thank you for everything that you've done for Mitzi."

"You don't have to thank me." She was embarrassed by his gratitude. "I'm only glad that we were able to help."

"You and your friend have helped more than you'll ever know."

Felicia's lips parted. She knew what she wanted to say, but she wasn't sure whether this was the place to say it or not. She wanted to tell him that God was the One who helped Mitzi get control of herself enough to get off of the cliff. But while she hesitated, the opportunity was gone.

"We want to talk with you and Joan when you get back to the resort."

Felicia nodded. "That will be fine. Joan and I will wait for you if we get there first."

For the space of a minute or more, he stood at the side of the jeep hesitantly, as though he had something else to say but wasn't sure quite how to say it. Then, changing his mind, he backed away.

"We'll see you in a little while at the resort."

The girls watched him go back to the jeep and get in with his wife and daughter.

"Did you see that, Joan?" Felicia asked, her excitement kindling once more. "They're all riding back to the lodge in the same jeep."

"I wonder if that means anything," Joan said.

"It means they're talking with each other, anyway. And that's an improvement."

Mrs. Rutledge came and got in the jeep, and the driver started the engine and pulled away.

"Wouldn't it be wonderful if they would get things

patched up between them? It would almost make what happened worthwhile, wouldn't it?" Joan asked.

"I suppose you're right," Felicia said, but as she thought of the ordeal she and Mitzi had just gone through, she shuddered. "I don't think I could go through it again though. It gives me cold chills just to think about it."

They drove on for the space of a mile or more before either spoke again.

"We'll have to pray that this time together will make Mitzi's parents realize that they do love each other and ought to get their differences resolved so they can reestablish their home and give her the love and care that she needs."

"I have been praying for them," Felicia said, "and I know that you have too."

Mrs. Rutledge, who was sitting in the front seat of the jouncing vehicle, turned around to get into the conversation.

"I had a long talk with Darlene Simmons while Mitzi was missing," she said, "and Clark is going to talk with John as soon as he has the opportunity."

That would be good, Felicia reasoned. Mr. and Mrs. Rutledge were old enough so Mitzi's parents could feel like confiding in them. They would know the sort of problems the estranged married couple faced. Maybe, just maybe, they would be able to make them see that they should go back together.

It was certainly something for her and Joan to be praying about.

Felicia hadn't realized how tired and hungry she was until they reached the lodge. Then it seemed that exhaustion swept over her, stealing the strength from her body. She wanted nothing more than to eat, go to their room, and sleep for a week.

But she had to wait and talk with Mr. Simmons. She had told him she would.

Mrs. Rutledge tried to talk her into going to bed anyway.

"I'll explain to Mr. Simmons when they get here," she said. "He'll understand."

"But I told him that I would see him as soon as he got back to the lodge," Felicia protested. "He's going to be expecting me."

They finally compromised by agreeing that they would wash up, then go into the dining room to eat; and if John Simmons wasn't back by the time they finished, Felicia was to go to bed.

"If he realized how tired you are, he wouldn't even want to talk to you until after you'd rested," Mrs. Rutledge insisted.

"I'm not so tired I can't wait for him," Felicia said. "But if you think it's best, we will do it your way."

"I think it's best," the woman said firmly.

The girls were just finishing a big meal when John Simmons came into the dining room looking for them. He stopped inside the door and looked around, his face lighting when he saw them.

"Oh, there you are," he said, approaching their table. "I was afraid that you had gone to your room."

"We were just finishing," Felicia said. "Won't you sit down?"

He pulled up a chair.

"Anita gave me strict orders not to bother you if you had gone to your room and not to stay here talking to you very long if I found you here. So I'll have to make it short."

"She sounds just like my mother about so many things," Felicia told him.

"I guess most girls need a mother to look after them."

Felicia and Joan eyed him quickly.

"What do you mean by that?"

His cheeks flushed.

"Nothing," he replied. "Nothing at all. I was just making conversation."

The momentary silence was painful.

"I wanted to come and thank you, personally, for what you did for Mitzi, Felicia," he said. "I was so excited about finding her alive and well that I didn't even think about how she got off the cliff until we were on our way back to the campsite with her."

Felicia's cheeks crimsoned. For some reason, his gratitude embarrassed her.

"I only did what had to be done."

"That's right. You only did what had to be done. And if you hadn't, Mitzi says that she would have fallen in a minute or two. She had been on the cliff so long that she hardly was able to hang on any longer."

"That's what I was afraid of. And she was so frightened, she was unable to move."

"Until you went out and came back with her," Mr. Simmons added.

"The important thing is that she's all right."

Mitzi's dad nodded, and for a time, he was silent.

"There's something else I've got to know, Felicia," he said, keeping his voice low. "Why did Mitzi run away from your camp in the first place? And why did she go out on that cliff?"

Felicia's gaze met his evenly.

"Don't you know?"

He shook his head. "No, and it's been bothering me a lot. It's not like her to do an irresponsible thing like that without a reason. She's not that kind of a girl."

"Well," Felicia pulled in a deep breath and expelled the air slowly. "It's not easy to tell you this, Mr. Simmons, but it was because of you."

"Me?" He jerked himself upright, his gaze boring into her. "Me? You've got to be kidding!"

"I'm telling you the truth. She thought you were going to South America to take a new job right away and that she would never get to see you again. So she decided to go down to the town of Silver City and call you before you left."

Mr. Simmons winced as though he had been slapped on the cheek. Then anger glittered in his eyes.

"Darlene's the one who did that!" he snarled. "I told her not to say anything about it to Mitzi yet! But she had to go and tell it! What happened was all her fault!"

Indignation flashed across Felicia's young face.

"*Was* it your wife's fault, Mr. Simmons?" she demanded. "Exactly what were you going to do? Did you plan to run away without even telling Mitzi goodbye?"

The corners of his mouth worked nervously, but he did not reply. By this time, the color had seeped from his cheeks, leaving his face ashen.

"Do you think it would have been any easier for your daughter to have you disappear and find out later that you'd gone to South America than to be told about it before you leave?"

He swallowed hard. "I–I couldn't stand to tell her," he stammered.

"So that's it!" Felicia's voice rose. "In other words, you weren't thinking about Mitzi at all. You were thinking about yourself. You didn't care how hard it was on her, just so it was easy for you."

He got to his feet stiffly, anger flecking his eyes.

"Thank you for what you did for Mitzi," he said, controlling his voice with difficulty. "We all appreciate it very much." With that, he pivoted and left.

Felicia and Joan stared after him. The Cartright girl was trembling.

"I–I didn't mean to say those things, Joan," she managed. "I don't know why, but they just popped out."

"They were things that needed to be said to him." Joan giggled. "I don't think I ever heard you tell off anyone like that before."

Felicia didn't think it was funny.

"I shouldn't have done it. I had no right to talk to Mr. Simmons like that."

When they left the dining room, Mitzi's dad was standing at the desk.

"I was going to stay for a few days, Clark," he was saying, "but I've changed my mind. Have one of the boys take my stuff to the car."

"I was hoping I'd have an opportunity to talk to you for a few minutes, John," the resort owner said.

"I've already had someone talk to me, thank you."

Felicia waited until he had finished at the desk and was leaving.

"Mr. Simmons?"

"Yes?" There was a thinly veiled warning in his voice that she be careful what she said to him.

"I want to apologize for what I said to you back in the dining room. I had no right to talk with you the way I did. I'm sorry."

"It's a little late for that now," he said testily.

Felicia was near tears when she and Joan got to their room.

"He wouldn't even accept my apology."

"You've apologized. If he doesn't accept it, that's his problem."

"I don't know why I talked that way about him. I feel terrible about it."

Joan kicked off her shoes.

"I don't know about you, but I'm going to worry about that *after* we've had some sleep. I'm exhausted!"

Felicia didn't think she would be able to sleep, but as soon as she closed her eyes, time blacked out. How long she slept, she didn't know, but it was dark in the room when she finally wakened.

"Joan?" She raised up on one elbow. "Joan?"

No answer.

She swung her feet over the side of the bed and reached for the light. It was past eight o'clock in the evening. Joan had probably gotten up and gone to dinner.

Felicia was suddenly aware of the fact that she was hungry herself. She would have to hurry, or she would miss out on dinner that night. They quit serving at nine.

She dressed hurriedly and went to the dining room. Joan was there, sitting with Mr. and Mrs. Simmons and Mitzi. She waved to Felicia and motioned her to the table, but John Simmons got up and went over to her.

"Hello, Felicia." His voice was apologetic.

"Hello. I–I thought you were leaving."

"I did, but I came back. Let's go into the lobby where we can talk." His voice was soft and conciliatory. "I am the one who has to apologize to you, Felicia. I'm terribly sorry that I lost my temper."

Her smile flashed.

"That's all right. I said things to you that were none of my business. I felt terrible after I said them."

"They were things that needed saying," he told her. "I got to thinking about what you'd said as I drove toward Silver City. I'd never realized it before, but I haven't been thinking of anyone else except myself."

Felicia did not say anything to break the silence that followed. There was nothing that she could say. After a time, Mr. Simmons continued.

"Finally, I turned around and came back here to talk with Darlene about our differences."

Felicia's spirits soared.

"And you got them straightened out?"

"Not exactly." His mouth hardened. "There are a lot of things we've got to get ironed out before things will be the way they used to be, but we've been talking with Clark and Anita Rutledge. They seem to feel that God's got the solution to our problems."

"I see," she said.

"I'm going to pass up this job in South America. I really didn't want to take it anyway. And when we get back to Pierre, we're going to look up a minister

Clark and Anita know there. I guess he does some counseling with people who have our kind of troubles."

"I'm so happy to hear you say that," Felicia said. "I'm sure you can get things worked out."

"I don't know about that," he said, "but I had a long talk with Darlene. We've both decided that we've got to think about Mitzi and each other instead of ourselves." He paused for a moment. "We're going to work at getting our differences resolved and at making a home for Mitzi."

Relief surged over Felicia.

"That's wonderful."

"And we may look into this Christianity business too. Mitzi was talking with us about the stand she's taken for God. It sounds as though it's exactly what we need."

Tears filled Felicia's eyes – tears of happiness. God was helping Mitzi to work out her problems. There was a prayer of thanksgiving in her heart as she went with Mr. Simmons to join Joan and his family.

THE
FELICIA CARTRIGHT
SERIES

Felicia Cartright, a petite blonde who is one of the most popular students at Wellington School for Girls, has a surprising inclination toward mysteries. If a mysterious situation arises, it either makes its way to Felicia, or Felicia somehow finds it. Though this is a bit trying for her happy-go-lucky roommate, Joan Bailey, it does prevent life from becoming monotonous. It also enables Bernard Palmer, the popular author of the "Danny Orlis" books, to write an entertaining series of stories for girls aged twelve to eighteen.

The mysteries range from a valuable missing antique to an attempt by claim jumpers to steal a deposit of tungsten ore. There's excitement and action galore—but there's also spiritual guidance and blessing because Felicia and her partner-in-adventure love the Lord and take Him into account in all their experiences.

AVAILABLE FROM WWW.ANEKOPRESS.COM